CONTENTS

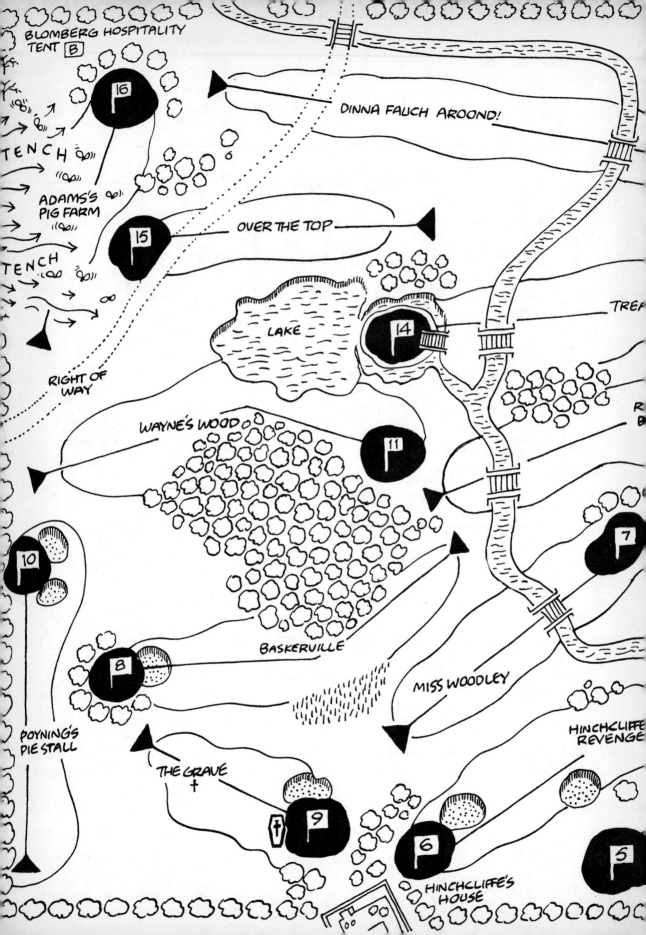

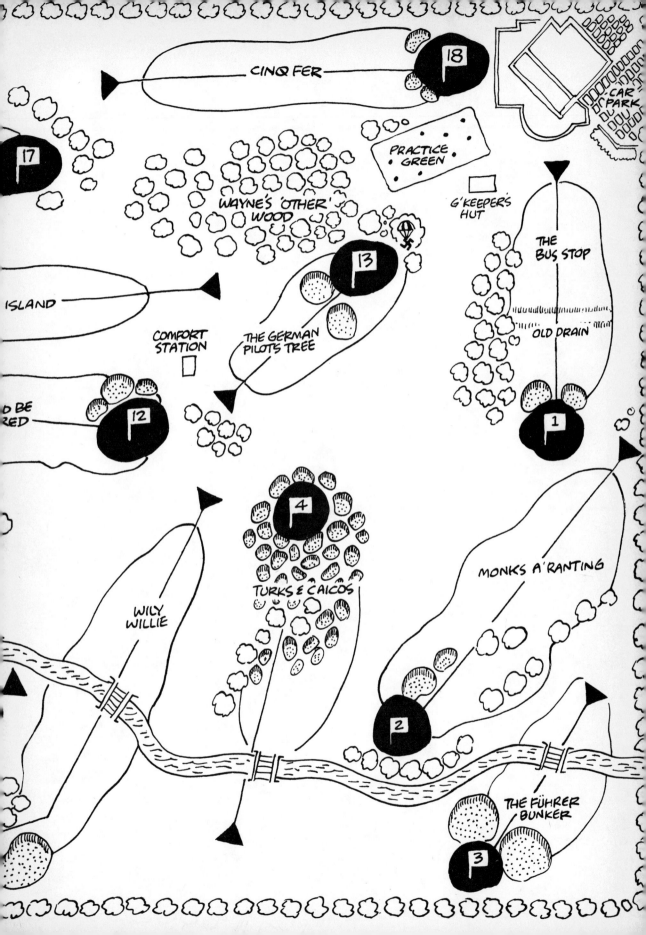

THE AGM

How Ralphie Jukes, President-elect, runs the Club, and why Len Gurning had to be reappointed Captain for the thirteenth successive year.

'Thank you, ladies and gentlemen.' Dear Old Jack Burberry rose unsteadily from the President's chair and waved like a drowning man for order. The trembling, ghostly hands had no effect on the members of Sheerpitts Golf Club Limited and the sounds of raucous laughter and golf scandal rose to a new crescendo.

Jack, managing director of Burberry's Brewery, and a major consumer of their brand leader, Monks a' Ranting bitter, had been hard at it since daybreak and had forgotten why he was here in the TV lounge of the golf club, faced by a mass of people all of whose faces were just out of focus. It was getting late for him still to be conscious, but he had a vague feeling that it was the first Saturday in October, or was it November, and that he should say something. Unaccustomed to standing unaided for longer than a pee, he just wanted to sleep. The swaying motion of his body became more pronounced; leaning heavily on the table didn't seem to help. Through the noise he heard a distant voice shout, 'Jack's going early. Grab him, Ralphie!'

Ralphie Jukes, builder, car dealer, things-off-lorries and President-elect, reached out and steadied the old man with his index finger. The sounds of the room died in admiration and the ghostly silence unnerved the brewer, who peered without hope at a point 18,000 miles away.

'Dear God,' rasped a bristling red-faced dwarf in the front row of chairs, and a chorus of groans presaged what was to follow. 'It's the AGM, Burberry, and I've got several points to raise.' Brigadier Gerald Patterson, VC, looked around angrily. 'So let's get on with the damn thing, what!'

The fruity, armour-piercing military voice penetrated Jack where Ralphie's probing finger had failed and, clinging desperately to his last functioning brain cell, the brewer gasped, 'Directors' Report and Accounts, Any Other Business,' then fell back in the President's chair and instantly left the meeting.

It was traditional at Sheerpitts AGMs to start this way and the sarcastic standing ovation was no longer than usual. Out of a total membership of 450, some 100 seats were occupied and, apart from the Brigadier and Margaret Vyner-Kenty, the Lady Captain who ate golf balls for breakfast, the main body of opinion simply wanted the whole tedious business over and done with as quickly as possible and back to the bar. Not only was precious drinking time being lost, there was always the distinct menace of being coerced onto some blasted committee and actually forced to do something unpaid.

A club membership made up of solicitors, accountants, doctors, scrap and car dealers, airline pilots, estate agents and bank managers did enough during the week – for God's sake! – dealing with the great unwashed public, without having to do more at playtime. Ralph Jukes, sensitive to the moods of professional men and safe in the sure knowledge that most of them were in his pocket anyway, looked up the table past Jack Burberry's straining

THE CLUB CAT

RALPHIE JUKES
(PRESIDENT ELECT)

CAPTAIN RHINO HUGHTON
(SECRETARY)

BRIGADIER
GERALD PATTERSON

LT COL.
R.S.J. BEAM
(TREASURER)

LEN GURNING
(CLUB CAPTAIN)

DEAR OLD JACK BURBERRY
(PRESIDENT)

waistcoat buttons and football medal, to the Club Secretary.

Captain 'Rhino' Hughton, RN Retired, was an extremely capable man and a relentless money-maker for Sheerpitts but his great genius was never to be there when required. He hated golf and golfers as much as he detested Freemasons and Mrs Tina Gurning, the Club Captain's wife. He was steadfastly looking out of the window to the clump of trees between the 7th,

MARGARET VYNER-KENTY
(LADIES CAPTAIN)

MARILYN

JOHN POTTS

AARON BLOMBERG

DR McNISH

ARCHIE GOSLING

ASST CHIEF CONSTABLE
KENNETH DOWTY

8th and 11th greens, known as Wayne's Wood, where he could confidently forecast that Wayne Summers, the assistant professional, would be going to town on a lady member or the lovely Marilyn Sidlow, daughter of Arthur, the vile and obsequious steward.

Ralphie sighed. He hated being a front man but someone had to keep the AGM moving. Jukes preferred to win his way by guile and deception, favour and obligation, sealing deals with drinks, reinforced on the nod by Arthur Sidlow. Now he rose to his feet. 'Ladies and gentlemen . . . in the absence of the President I'll ask you to receive and adopt the Directors' Report and Accounts . . .'

'Deceive and adopt!' the floor roared in time-honoured fashion.

'. . . the Directors' Report and Accounts for the year ended 31 May,' Ralphie went on. 'You all have copies and it's fairly straightforward, so can we have a proposer and seconder. Thank you, Harry.'

The accounts were in fact extremely complicated, though in no way dishonest or fraudulent. They were, however, very mobile, for, as Ralphie always said to Phasey, Weeks and Studholme, Accountants, a rolling bank account gathers no tax. Consequently, sums of Sheerpitts treasure financed lorryloads of things and the money was back in the bank before you could say Jack Burberry. What Jukes didn't want was the crimson brigadier poking his inflamed nose into private matters like the club accounts.

'What I'd like to know is just exactly what happens to our . . .' shouted the poison dwarf waving his copy of the year's trading. Dead on cue, the comatose brewer fell out of the presidential throne and the accounts were adopted before he had woken and fallen asleep again. The auditors were also reappointed, and as the Brigadier had nothing but searing contempt for the directors and officers of Sheerpitts, their re-election passed without a ripple.

'Right,' said Ralphie with a smile. 'That's J. Burberry President, Len Gurning Captain again, that's unusual but very nice considering . . . er . . . everything, R.B. Pews Vice-Captain, J. Potts, C.F. Winch, V.V. White and F. Rumsey. Thank you for your confidence which bears out the old adage: never change a whining team!'

The groans of horror at Ralphie's annual joke told him that the AGM was ticking over nicely. Dragging just a bit with some tetchy shifting in the hard seats, but the nasty part was over. With growing confidence he announced, 'I now call upon the Club Captain, Leonard Gurning, to give the Captain's Review. Len!'

The wearer of the red jacket, seated at the end of the table, rose, coughed, and faced the members. There was total silence. No chair creaked, coughs died in the throat and even 'Rhino' Hughton gave his full attention.

'Finance,' Len read from his notes. 'The Board adopted a policy of increasing income, up by £29,660 or 14%, with the subscription increase

Blomberg's Progress

'Aaron is a lovely boy, Mrs Blomberg. It's a great pity he never married. He would make some lucky girl a wonderful husband.'

'This I would like to see, Mrs Rabin, but I don't think so now.'

'Oh, Rachel, he's only in the prime of his life. There are lots of girls who would bring out the best in him. My own little Shula . . .'

'No, no, I mean he can never marry at present. He is doing something for his father. It will demand total dedication.'

'Rabbinical College!'

'More than that. He is taking up golf!'

'Golf . . . for his father? With *his* eyesight?'

'He has been made a member of Sheerpitts Golf Club.'

'And pigs can fly?'

'He is a member or I wouldn't say it!'

'I believe you, but how and why?'

'How is easy. We have a friend. Why is too deep for me. Blomberg wants him to do it and that's enough.'

'One of *us* in a golf club for Gentiles and Scotsmen?'

'Blomberg says the world needs a great Jewish golfer. We have actors, musicians, painters, scientists, tailors . . .'

'I didn't know he was interested in sport?'

'He is interested in everything. Blomberg met and mastered every obstacle he ever faced. He took prejudice without flinching or bearing resentment, but he knows that there is still too much hatred and suspicion in the world and sport is the answer. All men are equal on the sports field, so Aaron is mastering golf. In fact he's picking it up so fast he's on his fiftieth lesson!'

'I never thought of Mr Blomberg as a philosopher. He hides it so well.'

'All tailors are philosophers, Mrs Rabin. They know more about us than our doctors. Blomberg may look from the outside like a bitter cynic and God knows it's not been easy, but inside he's as soft as a matso ball.'

'And after the way he suffered. How is he?'

'So-so. It comes and goes.'

'His leg is troubling him again?'

'His leg that isn't there is troubling him again.'

HOLE 11
339 YARDS.
FOR ANYONE ELSE
PAR 4 BUT
FOR YOU 3

providing £11,473. The operating profits for the year . . .'

It was not the sheer gusto of his delivery nor his nit-picking concern for detail that had their unblinking, hypnotic attention. The origins of the new lounge carpet, and the two new table lamps, which he went on to describe at some length, passed them by completely. Coming from any other person, the Captain's blazing passion for Sheerpitts, his bleeding concern and obsessional love for the place would have elicited a storm of jeers and derision; but this was Len Gurning speaking. He of all men had their stony hearts, and that, thought Ralphie, looking around him, was certainly something!

The Club Captain was a fair golfer, a successful solicitor and stood his corner at the bar even when the arrival of the Brigadier caused the atmospheric phenomenon known as the 'Patterson Rush'. What drew the normally insensitive soaks of Sheerpitts to him was something which had occurred fourteen years before, not far from the club. On that ill-starred Thursday he had entered, alone, the Church of Saint Esmeric the Martyr in Bishop's Ranting, and had emerged 47 minutes later with his ravishing bride, Tina Gurning *née* Corker. Albertina Gurning was a rare beauty, and every man in the building, including the vicar and the saints in the niches, envied Leonard the lovely woman walking by his side. Her laughing eyes compelled the viewer to swim in them and the raven's wing of her blue-black hair accentuated the full lips and flawless complexion. Her generous figure caused women to bite their tongue and turn away in desolation, and sunshine and flowers seemed to spring from the very places where her tiny feet touched the ground.

After much pork and ham pie at the golf club and the reading of scandalous telegrams, the couple left for Madeira. It was there, in the home of the giant avocado, that it soon became apparent that God had given Saint Esmeric's a miss the previous day and that poor Len had coupled with the Medusa. Outwardly, Tina was breathtaking, a peach to be plunged into, but in truth the temple was built over a sewer. Had she been a deaf-mute, Len's life with her would have been short but memorable. Sadly his every moment with the Hydra, whether horizontal or vertical, was absolute purgatory. The wretch had married an acid-tongued, over-sexed, sharp-witted virago, whose only joy in life apart from any other man who could lay his hands on her, was to make her husband's existence a living nightmare.

Len would surely have slashed his wrists had he not almost immediately realized that the golf club was his bolthole. It was the only haven safe from the stinging aerosol of her terrible contempt, for she hated golf even more than she despised Len. What had happened on that terrible wedding night no other human being ever learned, although the gnarled Madeirans who guide tourists down the slopes in wicker baskets will, on payment of a few escudos, tell tantalizing stories of a bicycle pump being found in a hotel bed many years ago.

The golf club became Len's home and it was in the bar, the lounge, the locker-room or out on the course that the refugee learned to live the life of a golfing Quasimodo, with balls instead of bells as his only link with sanity.

'. . . projects in hand are the conversion of the trolley shed, and some alterations to the professional's shop to give a better display of equipment available.' Len stabbed out the vital information with ecclesiastical joy and verve. 'I express my appreciation for the great work done by the social committee, the filmed ostrich racing being one of the highspots of an interesting and eventful year. My reappointment as Captain for the thirteenth successive year is against my wishes but if it is the club's desire that I should take on the burden again . . .'

Poor bastard, everyone thought. Even those who craved the red coat of leadership could not find it in their hearts to send the poor devil back to that evil woman. Such feelings, although freely expressed, were not based entirely on philanthropic motives, for several members saw Mrs Gurning on a fairly regular and enjoyable basis and to have Len around would be embarrassing at the very least.

The hermit of Sheerpitts droned steadily to the end of his review, smiled happily and sat down in his licensed sanctuary for another precious year. He knew what they were all thinking. He's a solicitor, he's familiar with the law, so why doesn't he kill her. Solicitors get away with murder every day of the week. Conveyancing, court cases, conning old ladies. Heaven knows, thought Len, he'd considered it often enough, but what if he was found out! How many favours had it cost him getting Jukes to sweeten the membership into having him as their permanent captain, and also fixing up the cosy little sleeping shelf in the greenkeeper's hut when things became particularly hellish at 'Lenantinas', Long Ranting. It just didn't bear thinking about the amount of give and take it would need to coax Ralphie into squaring Assistant Chief Constable Kenneth Dowty to drop a murder charge. Dowty, though a keen member of the club, was a cold fish; a few weeks previously he had as much as admitted to fitting up Charlie Pringle for a burglary at the golf club . . .

Pringle, a well-known local breaking-and-entering specialist, though innocent on this occasion, was now a full-time boarder at HM Prison, Bracewell. Someone else had lifted the bottles of spirits and cigars from the bar, nicked the colour television and several cherished trophies including the Curtis Goblets. There had been, moreover, discontent among the lower orders of Bishop's Ranting New Town when the judge announced his verdict. The Pringles were a large and disorderly clan and there had already been much wailing and whingeing in the local newspaper about the affair. Len hoped that no scandal would reflect on his beloved club . . .

The Captain's reverie was shattered by the far-off but happy sound of the steward summoning the faithful to worship, laying out glass vessels of gherkins and crisps on the bar top. The room reaction was one of great relief and Ralphie responded quickly to the opportunity. He rose and coughed. 'Well, ladies and gentlemen, that appears to tie everything up for the present, and it only remains for the President to close.'

Jack Burberry's beer-clock had floated him almost to the surface and the old man began to struggle to his feet, but before he could assume a passable vertical the fiery Brigadier charged in. 'Any Other Business, dammit, we haven't got to Any Other Business. I thought this was supposed to be an AGM, dammit!'

'Oh, yes,' said Ralphie demurely. 'Is there Any Other . . . ?'

The Brigadier was in like a rat up a drainpipe. 'When is something going to be done about the man Adams and his confounded pigs? The stench is absolutely disgusting. Playing the 15th, the short 16th, where, incidentally, I holed in one yesterday morning, and teeing off at the 17th are an absolute nightmare.'

The old subject of Tom Adams and his appalling pig farm was a perennial sore, and no-one could do anything about the putrid air except hold their breath and run. The fact that the crimson war hero had holed in one surprised nobody, for he had accomplished the golfer's dream many times and always unaccompanied. Dear Old Jack was now in a state to respond.

'Have we had the Captain's Review yet, Ralphie?' he said in a loud clear voice. 'Oh, the bloody pig farm, is it. There's not a lot we can do about it, Brigadier. Ask the Secretary, he's the expert on foul smells.'

Captain Hughton showed his death's-head grin. 'No, Brigadier, not as long as there is no health risk or cruelty to the beasts. The piggery is inspected every quarter by ministry officers and vets and they tell me that he keeps it up to scratch. So, we'll keep on trying to close him down but I'm afraid that we haven't got much hope!'

Hughton spread his hands expressively and smiled again. Personally he never went within a mile of Adams and his pigs and he didn't care if the smell was bottled and sold as paint-stripper. The only time he was ever aware of the stink was in high summer when it would drift in gentle miasmic waves towards the clubhouse; even then all it did to him was bring back memories of his thirty years in HM Submarines and Chief Petty Officer Burkinshaw.

Ralphie waited. The Brigadier remounted and leapt in to the breach once more. 'We were solemnly promised last year that the subscriptions would remain as they were which was good news for those on pensions, like myself, and that the extra revenue would come from golfing societies. Is this really the way to run a first-class club? I'm sure that I was not alone amongst

Charlie's Campaign

The day after Charlie Pringle was awarded two years at Bishop's Ranting New Town Assizes, his family and friends met at the Rest and Be Buggered.

Over many pints of Monks, a plan of action was conceived to right the cruel injustice of an innocent thief being sent down for a job he had not pulled. Four independent but shy witnesses knew that Charlie could not possibly have done the golf club on the night in question because he was, in actual fact, twenty miles away at the time turning over Summer Ranting Conservative Club. The 'FREE CHARLIE PRINGLE CAMPAIGN' was launched and a full programme of eye-catching public demonstrations was decided upon.

Pakistan:

members in noticing that one of the persons from the New Town Abattoir Golfing Society was wearing bicycle clips on the course. Dear God!'

Ralphie felt a surge of impatience. Time was running out and he had seeds to plant. 'I'm sorry about dress irregularities, Brigadier,' he replied, 'we send out rules on apparel to all the societies that we accept to play here. Sometimes, I'm afraid . . .'

The rest of his sentence was instantly wiped away as an F15A from USAAF, Miles Ranting shrieked angrily over the clubhouse at 200 feet in a maniacal blast. The rolling thunder of its passing left the chandeliers tinkling. On every chairback white knuckles slowly coloured as the stupefying effect of the sound slowly diluted to distant grumbling, and terror changed to anger.

'Bloody Yanks!' cried Gerald Patterson, VC. 'Really, Mr President, we're paying a 9½ per cent increase in subscriptions and we've got American aircraft doing that every time they feel like it. When is some kind of representation going to be made to Colonel Ooks, who is not a bad person for an American, to explain to him our outrage?'

'I'm speaking to the Colonel tonight,' Ralphie said. He had a nice little ice cream and Log Cabin pancake syrup deal going at the base in exchange for Toby jugs and Spode rejects, and the principals were getting together over a drink that evening. 'I'll let him know exactly what our feelings are and report back to the House Committee. Now I think that . . .'

The desperate audience tensed like greyhounds as the steward's bar ballet now became a siren call, and collectively they willed the Brigadier to rot in hell if he opened his mouth again.

'The ladies' tees were appallingly sited last year. Is there any reason why less attention should be paid to the lady members' game than that of the other members?'

It was the Lady Captain. 'Each year, in spite of the unfair discrimination of the committee, I will continue to lodge a strong protest against the outmoded rules of this male dominated place which do not permit lady members to have voting rights at the AGM. Surely in the twentieth century . . .'

'Be satisfied that you're sitting here with us, woman, and give it a rest!' shouted the other members as one. Although it was expected, and happened regularly, the pain and humiliation never diminished. You bastards! she thought as they dismissed her and turned back to the chair, tongues hanging out appealingly. She fought for scraps. Margaret Vyner-Kenty's eyes smouldered as she set about demanding reparations.

'I'm used by now to living with boorishness and bad manners in the clubhouse, but the drunkenness on the course is too much to stomach. Several times recently it has been my great misfortune to encounter

Mr Gosling on the course in play. Is it not time that he be asked to accept medical attention or leave the club?'

Many heads turned to look at the object of her displeasure and contempt. Archibald Gosling sat comatose in his chair, loosely tied there in a friendly but secure manner. His chin was on his chest and in the long-lost Rubberlip language he was ordering a drink from a far-off invisible barman. Dr Murdo McNish now rose and spoke in the comforting burr that fills hospitals.

'Yes, Archie has a problem and I'll be glad to see him as a private patient anytime, but I don't think his condition is something to be discussed at the Golf Club AGM . . . especially *now!*'

He sat down heavily. Archie's problem was of course to do with drink. It was also undisputed by any person connected with Sheerpitts that he was the best golfer in the club. It was equally beyond doubt that Archie was the best golfer in the world. He had never completed a round on the course, which was a demanding test when the pig farm was on song, in more than 64 strokes, and he had on three occasions slaughtered the 6,340 yards in 61. Independent and impeccable witnesses were present on all three 61s including, on the last occasion, no less a person than the Captain of the R & A himself. All witnesses swore on their mother's grave that throughout the round the master had been totally legless, unable to mark his card or hit the ground with an umbrella, yet when pointed in the right direction with a club placed in his shaking hands, he had struck the ball exactly where he had wanted it to go.

However, the frantic excitement felt by most of the witnesses that a member of such an undistinguished club should be so blindingly talented, was swiftly quenched by the eminence from headquarters who, after observing the display in torrential rain and hurricane force winds, reprimanded Jack Burberry and said that no way was a drunk going to win the British and American Opens even though some had already tried and failed. No way!

None of this was ever communicated to Archie because he was always too far gone to talk to for any length of time, but the world's loss was Sheerpitts's gain, and it was a remarkable experience to push him over the course in his chair or in bad weather on a stretcher. With a bottle inside him, half a dozen in his bag and several more in trees and bunkers, the afternoon would pass joyously for all concerned, and another 61 would go into the record book.

'Untie him,' Jack now ordered. 'I'm not having any more of this. It's been a long hard day and maybe we can impose on Sidlow to dip into the special fund . . .'

This time it was Ralphie's turn to play his joker. 'There's just one final thing.' 'Oh, for God's sake!' shouted a desperate McNish, but Ralphie

A TYPICAL ARCHIE GOSLING PAR 5 HOLE PLAYED WALKING.

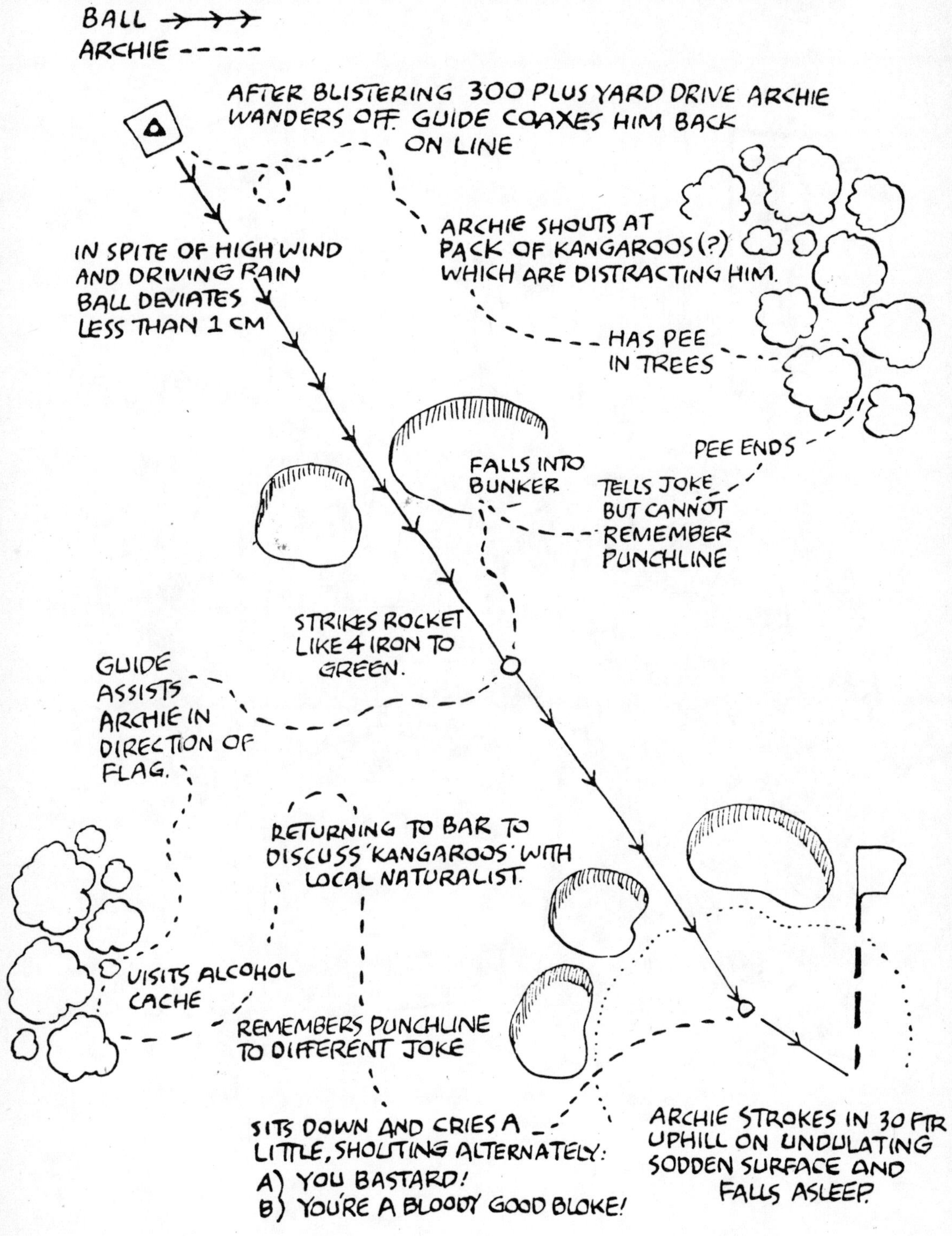

BALL →→→
ARCHIE -----

AFTER BLISTERING 300 PLUS YARD DRIVE ARCHIE WANDERS OFF. GUIDE COAXES HIM BACK ON LINE

ARCHIE SHOUTS AT PACK OF KANGAROOS (?) WHICH ARE DISTRACTING HIM.

IN SPITE OF HIGH WIND AND DRIVING RAIN BALL DEVIATES LESS THAN 1 CM

HAS PEE IN TREES

FALLS INTO BUNKER

PEE ENDS

TELLS JOKE BUT CANNOT REMEMBER PUNCHLINE

STRIKES ROCKET LIKE 4 IRON TO GREEN.

GUIDE ASSISTS ARCHIE IN DIRECTION OF FLAG.

RETURNING TO BAR TO DISCUSS 'KANGAROOS' WITH LOCAL NATURALIST.

VISITS ALCOHOL CACHE

REMEMBERS PUNCHLINE TO DIFFERENT JOKE

SITS DOWN AND CRIES A LITTLE, SHOUTING ALTERNATELY:
A) YOU BASTARD!
B) YOU'RE A BLOODY GOOD BLOKE!

ARCHIE STROKES IN 30 FTR UPHILL ON UNDULATING SODDEN SURFACE AND FALLS ASLEEP.

would not be stopped. 'I'm sorry, but it's important. Can I have your attention for just a couple of seconds. I'd like your views on us hosting a Pro-Am Celebrity tournament here at Sheerpitts.'

All around the room the looks of naked hatred froze and there was a general hesitation and curiosity. 'Big names. Top players and all the showbiz crowd. I'm sorry to leave it so late but I think it's a great idea and it would give the club press coverage, and I expect the TV would be here. It ties in with Cooper's benefit year and as well as seeing him off it could pay for ground improvements and probably keep subs down for quite a while.'

There was a buzz of approval and Ralphie knew he had them. 'Look, it's too late to discuss it properly now. Why don't I knock out an outline plan and distribute it to all members and set up a committee to hear your views. We could meet in a month. Show of hands.'

A forest of sweating palms faced Ralphie, and Dear Old Jack added his, shouting, 'I declare this Annual General Meeting of Sheerpitts Golf Club closed. Thank you, ladies and gentlemen.'

Like a rock in the demented torrent flooding towards the haven of the bar, Aaron Blomberg stood, fat and determined with his arms raised as in Old Testament days. 'What about the fall in standards of dress as referred to by the General?'

McNish bounced off him, 'The meeting's over and we're all very dry, but I don't expect you'll be buying.'

'I do a very nice club blazer with gold badge,' added Aaron but it was useless. McNish was past him in a whirl of tweed and the room was emptying fast. Soon only the Brigadier remained, ostensibly sorting his papers but in actual fact working out his point of attack at the bar. The Patterson Free Drink Principle was to let them get thick and confident and onto their second before arriving stealthily amongst them and slapping the victim heartily on the back. They would be ready for him, by God he knew that, but so were the Japs at Mandalay and he'd skinned those little buggers. Yes. Gosling, Potts, Gurning and the little balding chap were in a careless animated bunch. Those miserable Jocks had moved from the bar and were in their usual hiding place by the window, and the other members were spread out at tables, so it would have to be the bar. He'd give them another minute and then he'd pounce.

The AGM was over; life was back to normal.

Blomberg's Progress

Aaron Blomberg was on his 51st lesson with Norman Cooper, the Sheerpitts professional, who was beginning to feel that perhaps his benefit year wasn't going to be too bad after all. Before the new pupil's arrival the club members had studiously ignored the collecting boxes placed strategically in every place where a man or woman might pause for breath, and the take was minimal.

Cooper had been considering self-immolation to advertise that this was supposed to be the year when grateful students and purchasers of his overpriced golf equipment would help to make the twilight of his retirement tolerably alcoholic by voluntary contribution. In practice this had not happened, as in his heart of hearts he knew it would not. 'The mean, tight-arsed bastards,' he had said to Wayne every day since the generous offer of a benefit year had been accepted. 'There's a spiders web on the collecting box in the spike bar. I'll get nothing from this lot – after all I've given the bloody place.'

Norman had given the club nothing that could not have been purchased at half the price at the golf section of the Sports Hypermarket in the New Town. But now Aaron had come along with the ideal attributes of a good learner. Perfect lack of muscular and mental coordination, but total

determination to attempt the impossible at whatever cost. In other words, Cooper's pension.

'I'm a bit worried about those trousers, Mr Blomberg. They could be too tight and affecting your swing. Let's try again'.

It was 0745 on a Tuesday morning and the commencement of Aaron Blomberg's third period of instruction since dawn. The Genesis start was due to the Pro-Am Charity Tournament Committee's decision to present a Knockout Competition Vase, to be played for by the members. The trophy, which depicted a stunted figure attempting to commit ritual suicide on the handle of a driver, would be awarded to the survivor of an elimination competition, and the winner would also have the honour of partnering a Superstar on the day of the tournament. Blomberg had instantly trebled his contributions to the professional's retirement nest-egg, and to explosive laughter from the

barflies put his name down for the Vase. The jeers turned to stunned incredulity when he survived his first encounter in competitive golf and earned a place in the second round with 63 others.

'I can see you out there with Trevino and Sean Connery yet, Mr Blomberg,' Norman said as he watched his protegé slice his fifth Norman Cooper 666 into Sheerpitts Brook. The bulky figure searching in his bag for another sacrifice to Poseidon waved a hand dismissively. Finding an elderly ball he bent, placed it on the ground and patiently addressed it as Cooper moved in, tut-tutting to correct the podgy fingers of his right-hand overlap. The five-second backswing presaged a woodpecker rattle as the ball ricochetted through the trees beyond rescue.

'You moved your head. How many times do I have to tell you?'

Aaron dropped the club on the ground and entwined his fingers. 'It's hopeless. I can't get it. They queue up to watch me tee off on the 1st.'

Norman picked up the club and handed it back to Aaron. 'It is not hopeless. When you're out with me sometimes you string two good shots together, and that's very good after twenty lessons . . .'

'Fifty lessons!'

'Who gave you any chance against Sandy Moran? Was there one man in the club apart from me who said that you could do it?'

'No, but . . .'

'Are you in the second round or is Sandy?'

'I am, but . . .'

'Mr Blomberg, I am going to be completely honest with you. Your problem is nerves and that affects concentration. I am a Yorkshireman and we are known for our bluntness. We don't bugger about. I'm telling you that you are more worried about having a fat arse and being a Jew than you are about how far you are going to hit the ball! All you can think about is other people laughing at you and making comments. Instead of playing the course you're playing every member in the club!'

Aaron's face was crimson and he wiped it with a large white handkerchief. He seemed close to tears. 'What am I going to do, Mr Cooper?'

Norman looked carefully at his pupil. If he didn't come up with some effective advice soon, his best-ever source of income might well dry up without further notice. 'Look, Mr Blomberg,' he said. 'Why don't you look at some of the other members and see how they play. Take the Brigadier. Do you think he is a good golfer?'

To this question his pupil had no doubts at all. 'No, he's a cheat. Nobody believes his crazy claims.'

The professional smiled wisely and shook his head. 'That's where you're wrong. He's a great golfer because he's conquered the course without actually playing it . . .'

'No, no,' cried Blomberg, waving his arms in agitation. 'He farts just as you are about to putt!'

'Exactly, Mr Blomberg. It's gamesmanship! He breaks your shield of application. After that you ignore the course and start playing him – and you're kettled. It's like Trevino's jolly quips. They shield him and psyche the opponent. They all do it. Farting may not appeal to everybody but it's the technique best suited to the Brigadier and he uses it to the utmost advantage.'

Aaron seemed dazed and leaned back on his trolley. 'But you're talking about Sport. You are saying that there's more to it than the ball and clubs and the weather . . .'

Cooper stopped him with a finger and, taking Aaron's golfing umbrella from the trolley threw an old ball down and struck it into the trees with the stubby handle. 'That's a trickshot and don't ever let me see you try it. My friend, we could all play with umbrellas or walking sticks or anything you care to name, but that would blow the gaffe. The mystery would be gone. Only a few of us, and from today that includes you, know that it is not a game, and even at this level here in Sheerpitts certain of our number treat it as importantly as life itself. And there's only one way to play life. The Brigadier's way. Call it gamesmanship, cheating or whatever, but without it you might just as well not start.'

The professional paused. 'I'm going to have to find some kind of protective shield for you. What about that funny singing they do in your church. The Rabbi sort of chants in the back of his throat. Try that when you address the ball and you'll have the opposition reeling.'

Blomberg was unhappy. 'I don't know, Norman . . .'

'It's your choice, Mr Blomberg. I can only teach you so much. If you want to win the Vase and maybe walk Sheerpitts with Seve Ballesteros . . .'

The words seemed to be written in the air, and two inches below Aaron's tonsils the 'Prayers for the Dead' began to shape into a golfing defence. Strange he should think first of the dead, but perhaps it was a sign! After his unexpected victory in the first round of the Vase – A. Blomberg defeated A. Moran, deceased (walkover) – anything was possible.

THE HISTORY OF SHEERPITTS

How a select band of solicitors, doctors and army officers built and fortified their earthly paradise.

First some statistics. Sheerpitts golf course is 34 miles north of London, four miles from Bishop's Ranting New Town, and it is 6,379 yards and 22 paces from the 1st tee to Mrs Sidlow's shivering 42 inches behind the bar in the clubhouse.

In pre-Roman times Bishop's Ranting had simply been Ranting to the Druids and their wicker-caged sacrifices for the forest gods. St Esmeric the Martyr had introduced Christianity in 541, and homage is still paid to him every day of the year at Sheerpitts where Jews continue to be refused membership of the club. An Abbey was built on the spot where the gentle 89-year-old monk was bounced to death seated on a Viking helmet. Here the brothers, taken by the purity and tanginess of the local water, started to brew beer. On the appointment of Gribo the Abbot to the Bishopric of Ranting, the town became Bishop's Ranting. The town grew and survived the Black Death thanks to chains of holy bungs sold from the Abbey, worn around the drinking arms of the faithful.

While the Plague of 1665 destroyed upwards of 100,000 souls (one from Long Ranting) and London's Great Fire of 1666 reduced two-thirds of the metropolis to ashes, the most remarkable happening in the Rantings was Algernon Poyning, the Fat Boy. Thirty-six dozen meat pies at a sitting, washed down with a firkin of Monks, were nothing to him. 'Poyning' is still used by the locals as a term denoting great urgency, e.g. an anxious rattling at the latch of an occupied outside toilet – 'He's poyning a bit, then.'

The town slumbered until the Industrial Revolution when money pulled the workers into London, and filth drove the owners out. Successful factory owners and professional men, anxious to escape the capital's noxious effluent, took to the country. The unsure stopped at Hampstead and Finchley but the more resolute ploughed on. Thirty miles was a vast distance in those days but the gritty pioneers who eventually took root amongst the yokels of the Rantings were the forbears of the Sheerpitts membership today.

The area became 'select' and wealthy, but never 'country'. The local gentry at first tried to ignore the new people, and when that failed they retired into madness and incest. For their part the pioneers never rode to hounds or played polo. They could only offer middling, steady, unimaginative wealth allied to the authority of solicitors, doctors and the military. All that was needed to ensure ideal conditions for the founding of a golf club was the addition of professions as yet unheard-of, but coming: estate agents, scrap merchants, property developers and airline pilots.

Bishop's Ranting and its attendant nestlings, Much Ranting, Miles Ranting, Lower, Upper, Gone and Girt Ranting, passed quietly through

OBLIGATORY POEMS FOR OFFICERS

World War I. The area's single casualty was the 6th Rantings, a regiment of bumpkins who disappeared almost without trace in fog between Paris and Mons in 1915. It was at Mons that the only survivor, Colonel Anthony Bagyard-Dawes, MC, CO of the 6th, alleged that he had witnessed the Great War Phenomenon known as the Angels of Cinq Fer. This had been seen by nearly a million men on both sides of the grassless pitted waste over which the panoramic display appeared. To each weary soul bathed in the

unearthly glow of the dancing, flickering luminescence lighting up the night sky, the sight meant something different. For Tommy and Fritz, who had seen nothing more beautiful than plum and apple jam for a year, it was enough to gape in awe as children. The watching meteorologists smiled and said that it was a freak aurora, quite common after humid weather followed by heavy rain, and nudged each other as the poets slipped into their private trenches and wrote of divine displeasure and their mothers. Of all the observers it was to Colonel Bagyard-Dawes that the most earth moving revelation came. In the split second before a German shell almost completely buried him he saw a scene which remained burned into his memory for ever. The countless sucking craters, the endless mud and a splintered tree below while above, the brilliant colours and – oblivion. At the first aid post, the field hospital and even in the little Nieces of the Jebus Hospice 'Officers Section' he still cried in delirium that the heavens were full of angels at play, and that if he was spared, the sole purpose of his remaining days would be to build a soft green cathedral in memory of the murdered fields, fill the shell holes with the sand of the sea shore and erect a fluttering yellow flag for each dead tree.

The memory of the sterile cratered moonscape stayed with him after he lost a leg and was invalided out in 1916. Hating flowers, shrubs, lawns and, particularly, ornamental ponds with ducks on them, Anthony decided that he would organize the designing and landscaping of a golf course near his birthplace, Bishop's Ranting. Furthermore, and out of the goodness of his heart, he ordained that he would only employ one-legged ex-servicemen on the project.

Thousands limped to his call, for these were desperate times, and some, frantic for work, even abandoned their remaining limb to gain preference. The first sod was turned in March 1917 at Sheerpitts, several miles south-east of Bishop's Ranting. The project met with great acclaim from charitable institutions and hospitals, but some opposition from the 19 dance halls in Bishop's Ranting, 18 of which had closed by the year's end. On 17 July 1920 the enterprise was completed and Sheerpitts Golf Club lay green and bunkered around Colonel Bagyard-Dawes's home, 'Mons'. The official opening was marred by the good soldier's death, from an infarct, but his timely departure was toasted by all and club officers were appointed. His home became the clubhouse and a constitution was smartly composed barring one-legged men from the course forever. The ban applied also to one-armed men, because the presence of so many limbless ex-servicemen had offended the new committee and it was decided that, in future, the club would only embrace 'complete' people of an accepted profession. The exceptions to the rule would be pushy, vulgar men whose wealth would buy them acceptance. It was now that the estate agents, property developers and scrap merchants came in from the cold.

Sheerpitts is hard to find, intentionally so. Its location was deliberately kept obscure, ensuring that in the beginning only those able to afford a motor vehicle would be able to reach it. Bishop's Ranting Brown Bus Service terminates its No 7 route at March Ranting, three miles away from the club down Sheerpitts Lane. The absence of public transport guaranteed safety from that most obnoxious of golfing types, he who arrives on foot. Bicycles had been banned from the one-legged workforce days, and the club's isolation was complete.

This was a great comfort during the Depression, for the world slump had no effect. From the cosiness of the clubhouse it was impossible to see Jarrow or the Lancashire cotton towns, and the talk was about golf, cricket, plum trees and, of course, holing in one. The conversation is much the same today, for as yet the golfer's dream has become a nightmare at Sheerpitts. In 67 years and 1½ billion strokes, no tee shot has directly troubled the cup. Not officially. Brigadier Gerald Patterson, VC, a present member, has accomplished the feat 17 times, unaccompanied. The fiery war hero and dwarf is a cheat of fiendish ingenuity and no-one in the club believes a word

STILL THE COMIC
EH, NIBLOE!

he says. His VC is genuine, earned in Burma at Mandalay when he slaughtered dozens of Japs, many taller than himself.

In the same war, golf architect Hermann Goering redesigned the 156 yard 3rd. Two 50kg bombs turned a simple par three into a hellish seven for those powerless to the allure of sand traps.

The blazing Dornier Do-17 responsible for the new obstacles crashed on to Adams's pig farm near the 15th. The sole survivor, the pilot, was found in a tree on the 13th fairway, and taken by the club professional, Price, armed with a pitching wedge, to the clubhouse. Choice of club had bothered Price before he set out to capture the German, for he had consistently underclubbed all his life. He chose a 5-iron for the Luftwaffe and then, fearing that the parachutist might carry a pistol, he'd gone for the heavier metal. The pilot surrendered quietly but then, on the steps of the clubhouse, turned to Price and reminded him that, as a professional, he was not allowed inside but that he would arrange for a cup of tea to be sent out. Price kicked him and was dismissed on the spot for showing discourtesy to a guest of the club. The two new traps became known as the Führer Bunker and the Kick in the Arse.

The Dornier blazing on Adams's piggery filled the hearts of the members with great joy – partly for patriotic reasons but mostly because the smell of burning fuel and rubber, added to the acrid fumes of exploding cordite, was the sweetest odour ever to issue from that direction. Their pleasure was ruined when, despite the town fire engine breaking down en route to the show, Adams himself put an end to the conflagration by emptying a load of carrots onto the wreck. To compound the felony of claiming and being awarded a grossly exaggerated damages claim, Adams was decorated with the George Medal for bravery. The smell in the area, and particularly around the 10th green, intensified, and not even 'Twitchy' Pomfret, King of the Short Ones, took more than two to get down. The 15th tee, much closer to the porcine hell, became a Le Mans start and running was permitted.

The Americans came to the Rantings in 1960. RAF Ranting had been in operation since the Thirties but had never been more than a retirement home for the dangerously incompetent. In World War II, it had been closed in order not to attract attention to the treasures, relics and garb of the Grand Lodge of All England which were buried for safe keeping nearby in the cellars of Burberry's Brewery in Bishop's Ranting. After the war, the RAF tried to carry on as before but economic stringencies meant the mothballing of the establishment. That could have been the end of Ranting aviation had not the USAAF become aware of the field's tremendous strategic importance, and its closeness to the bright lights of London.

USAAF Miles Ranting became home to 800 men, all except for the CO banned permanently from the golf club but allowed out at any time to visit

London. The only occasion any American visits Bishop's Ranting is to go to the Rest and Be Buggered for a warm beer. They stare at the town's stunningly plain girls, then at the drunken teachers and local craftsmen, most of whom are bookbinders, and are carried unconscious back to the base in the Provost Marshall's wagon. Colonel Alvin Ooks, USAAF base commander, is an *ex-officio* club member and supplies steward Arthur Sidlow with ice cream. No other United States officer or enlisted man gets nearer than 200 feet to the luscious greens and fairways, which they do every day as they blast over in their maniacally screaming F15As.

It was all so different in 1945. The war ended and the boys came home to a Labour victory at the polls. This unmitigated catastrophe, the worst in the club's history, ended for all time the naive notion that a land fit for heroes had anything in common with membership of Sheerpitts Golf Club. Qualifications for membership, already brutal in their simplicity, were not deemed restrictive enough in a climate rank with Socialists, school dinners and the NHS. In 1947 an extra extraordinary AGM was called and a Rules of Membership Committee was appointed to 'clarify certain anomalies'. Under the leadership of 'See 'em Off' Balderstone, High Court Judge, Club President and whizz on contract law, a proper exclusivity was established which has prevailed to this day. Anyone doubting the efficacy of the new Rules of Membership is invited to apply to join the club – and see what happens if you are paid weekly.

Socialism was held safely at bay, and despite the insidious spread of the motor car the club managed to preserve its privileged isolation. Each year, like climbing poppies, the photographs of proud, serious red-coated Club Captains progressed further along the walls of the clubhouse. The honours boards lengthened and the names of golfing tigers made neat columns of consonants and vowels.

> 1959-60 The Curtis Goblets   Y.E.P. Pottleton-Veal
> 1960-61 The Curtis Goblets   Y.E.P. Pottleton-Veal
> 1961-62 The Curtis Goblets   Y.E.P. Pottleton-Veal
> 1962-63 The Curtis Goblets   Y.E.P. Pottleton-Veal
> 1963-64 The Curtis Goblets   Y.E.P. Pottleton-Veal
> 1964-65 The Curtis Goblets   Y.E.P. Pottleton-Veal
> 1965-66 The Curtis Goblets   Y.E.P. Pottleton-Veal
> 1966-67 The Curtis Goblets   Y.E.P. Pottleton-Veal

The waviest line on the Sheerpitts Richter Scale, after the '10' of the Labour takeover in 1946, was the New Town Affair. The building of the New Town was a direct insult, planned, aimed and executed in a fit of pique by Samuel Hinchcliffe, earth mover and builder of Blackburn, Lancashire. Recovering in the vicinity from a nasty accident, he had purchased a large house actually encroaching on the 6th green. The vendor had assured his agent that it was traditional for the owner-occupier to be given club membership, and this pleased Sam.

He paid over the odds for the house but, ever-cautious, made inquiries at the club about the truth of the tradition. Sam's vast wealth laundered the offputting impression given by his foul tongue and boorish manner, and the Membership Committee were delighted to hint, off the record, that the fallacious story was perfectly true. Sam was a thug, but he was smart enough to appreciate that Sheerpitts was not Central Lancashire. Racing pigeons would be as 'out' as pitch and toss, cock fighting and leg strings, so he

The Rantings on World Stage in Political Storm!

by Hilton Pocock, Our Chief Political Reporter

A major international row which could endanger the forthcoming Moscow Summit meeting reached boiling point yesterday with fierce Home Office and Soviet repudiation of my sensational World Exclusive in the New Town Examiner on Monday regarding the whereabouts of 49-year-old Oleg Federentsev.

On BBC television last night Lord Parsleigh for the government referred to his statement of the previous day and said that as far as he knew Mr Federenstev was what he said he was, an accredited journalist with the London office of Tass, and had done nothing to incur the displeasure of the Security Services.

GUTTER INVENTION

If there was a mystery it was purely a domestic matter for the Russians although his own feelings were that the report was gutter invention of the worst kind and all the more unfortunate in its timing with the East-West conference so imminent.

Later on ITV the Soviet Embassy Press Attaché, Mr Simyon Levtushenko, angrily denied my allegations that Mr Federentsev had been depressed and considering defecting to the West, that he had gone to St Pancras station, boarded a train at random and while resting at a retreat in The Rantings area had disappeared late on Sunday night in the company of three men.

Mr Levtushenko dismissed the story as utter fabrication and said that Federentsev had expressed a wish to return home to see his ailing mother, and had left on a scheduled Aeroflot Moscow flight the previous Wednesday. He had no idea how Oleg Federentsev's name had become involved in the other version of events. He assumed that it was because he was a well-known figure around London, wore a distinctive bushy moustache and appeared regularly on British television.

TWO NIGHTS

I can reveal that Oleg Federentsev did indeed spend two nights in Bishop's Ranting New Town. I have sworn depositions from reliable witnesses claiming that they encountered the Russian, alone and weeping on the banks of Hinchcliffe Canal on Saturday afternoon, and how, out of compassion and not knowing his identity, they took him home for a bath and a meal. Late that evening he poured out his heart to them.

My sources clearly recall his bitterness at the treatment of dissidents in the USSR and particularly his sorrow for those imprisoned for long terms on trumped-up charges. Shown photographs of Federentsev, the 63-year-old housewife who cooked his last meal of fish fingers, peas and chips, said, 'Yes, that is the man who was dragged screaming from our house which is the last one in Hinchcliffe Gardens, the one with the big board outside with the petition nailed to it, surrounded by those awful reporters.

'My husband Frank begged them to let the man go but was cuffed to the carpet, as was my daughter Fenella, 22 and an exotic dancer. He was a nice man, God help him, for we of all people know full well how he feels about the wrongfully imprisoned, which does not only occur in the Soviet Union. My own darling boy, Charles Everett Pringle, is at this very moment languishing in prison, banged up for something he did not do!'

The Pringles and their large family sit quietly at home, fearful that their telephone is tapped and that the house is under 24-hour watch. When I spoke this morning by telephone to the MP for The Rantings, Sir Harold Wing, he said, 'How typical that all stories emanating from The Rantings, be they true or false, are based 100 per cent on the warmth and kind-hearted generosity to strangers for which the area is renowned.

SALT OF THE EARTH

I myself have never been less than totally overwhelmed by their instant acceptance and hospitality to outsiders. They are the salt of the earth, and while I cannot of course comment on Federentsev until I have spoken to Lord Parsleigh I will certainly highlight the Pringle case when the House reassembles in two weeks.'

In my two months as a crusading political journalist, offering and accepting favour from no man, I have come across many baffling mysteries but this one surely must rank with the Marie Céleste and the Bridge over the River Kwai for sheer complexity and Oriental intrigue. Will we ever know what was behind the Federentsev Affair? Tomorrow. The locked room at No. 10 Downing Street.

entered the dining room on that first and last visit with a certain modest stillness and humility. He was immediately approached by the Secretary and asked courteously to leave his dogs outside in the car park. Tess, the gentle labrador guide dog, was faintly tolerable, but the pair of ghostly trembling whippets, and the bulldog grimly urinating on the carpet, were too much.

When the incredulous millionaire finally realized that the Secretary was not joking, he flailed wildly with his stick and, knocking over four tables and panicking the dogs, stormed out never to return. The Committee had allowed its greed to override any queries as to why a blind man should wish to join a golf club, and in a way were sad to see him stagger off with a shattering of glass through the closed bay window.

Their feelings changed two days later, when Hinchcliffe announced his philanthropic scheme to build 33,000 houses in the area, for the scum of the capital, and to call this sink Bishop's Ranting New Town. All attempts to stop him, in the brave new Socialist Britain, failed and the houses, red and box-like, spread like scrofula over the countryside. Prices and rents were very low, but Sam's design was not entirely benevolent. He simply wanted to lure the dregs of London's slums to the town, where they would be encouraged to take up golf. He prayed that after the pubs closed on Sunday, they would tuck their trousers into their socks, lurch drunkenly up to Sheerpitts and demand to hire clubs or wreck the place.

It didn't happen. Bishop's Ranting New Town behaved exactly like all new towns before and since. It was thought in those happy naive days that to give a spurious plantation of homes a ridiculous name would endow it with the reality of a Wigan, Barnsley or Walsall. It was not to be. The criminals who designed the chimera lived as far away from their aberration as was possible. Bishop's Ranting, or BR as it came to be called, was as big and useless as a diplodocus and, had it not been for Monks a' Ranting beer, would have followed the other dinosaurs into extinction. It had no football team of note, nor any that played chess, cricket, rugby, lacrosse, bowls, darts, snooker, morris dancing or ludo. There was no museum, decent newspaper, joke shop or red-light district. Nothing. Its clergymen never ran off with Boy Scouts and no mass murderer stacked crates in his saner moments on its wretched industrial estate.

BR's schools, cinemas, shops, one remaining dance hall and youth clubs were hardly used by the listless grey souls who peopled the necropolis. The gutter element of London easily resisted BR's pull and stayed put, leaving the New Town to its teachers and bookbinders. BR seemed to be populated entirely by teachers with leather elbows and bookbinders with red-stained fingers. Forefathers of the latter had founded their Guild in the town in 1668, and shortly afterwards produced their first work, a burgundy-bound edition of *Poyning's Undoing,* a history of gluttony.

Only the beer saved the somnolent and resolutely mediocre town from a decent burial. Every night the Rest and Be Buggered throbbed, packed with drunken teachers and dusty bookbinders boring each other to death. Sam Hinchcliffe's Great Revenge failed miserably, for not one new Rantonian had the courage, wit or inclination to march up to the verdant acres. Severely piqued, the old man sold the house on the 6th, and after ordering his butler to turn over the green at dead of night with a JCB, headed North where people did not object to pets. His last philanthropic and venomous gesture was to build an asylum near his home town, and it was in the Sheerpitts Home for the Understandably Insane that he died, a howling lunatic, two years later. Today there are members who say that, on the anniversary of the time the dog watered the carpet, sounds can be heard. Others, less romantic in their approach to the grim realities of life and love, say that the noises can be heard most of the summer and put them down to young Wayne Summers, the assistant pro, showing a lady student the Vardon grip.

Today the club prospers and, with the exception of Aaron Blomberg, only the right people cluster round the spike bar. The Scottish contingent still gather in poisonous clumps, complain bitterly about everything English from toilet paper to bunker sand, and still want to know why they can't get a toasted cheese sandwich at 2.30 in the morning. They live only for the day when, once a year at Sheerpitts, Scotland takes on the Rest of the World.

As the day approaches, they pray that it dawns with drenching rain, which it always does. They always win because they are better golfers than the rest of the club and, furthermore, Archie Gosling, the club's best player, always changes nationality to the land of his drink, just for the day. The English majority don't give a damn about the match itself and count the annual defeat as a small price to pay for the pleasure of getting a free drink out of McNish and Co. As ever, they laugh too loudly, tell filthy jokes and expect total silence when they read the *Telegraph*. The Membership Committee brooks no school teachers and the clipped home-county vowels are never shamed by the lilt of Caedmon. Colonel Alvin Ooks, USAAF, is, as previously mentioned, a member of the club for no other reason than to keep the number of shrieking overflights per day at a tolerable level. The anger caused by the overflights is assuaged a little by Ooks's friendly and servile manner and, of course, by his ridiculous Southern drawl. No other nationality is represented at Sheerpitts apart from an Irishman who delivers potatoes to the kitchen, and that is exactly how it should be.

OI'L BRING THE OTHER ONE TOMORROW

Blomberg's Progress

The tree hit the postman and he spilled from his bicycle in a confetti of flying envelopes, but still with the image of Tina Gurning's rock-firm breasts and the straining shot silk etched into his retinas. She was standing at the garage door in a clinging dressing gown shouting at someone inside.

'Why the hell does it have to be today? You knew that Annabel and Heinz were coming. When will you be back?'

Her husband was too terrified to face her and spoke directly to the spare tyre in the boot as he loaded his clubs and trolley. 'It's the Vase, love. I'm obliged to enter, but today won't take long. I've been drawn against the Wandering Jew. Shouldn't take more than an hour and a half. Promise!'

The postman handed Mrs Gurning a bunch of letters and instantly the anger faded from her face and she bathed him in a look which misdirected all further deliveries that day. He lurched away and she was her viperous self again. 'You'd better be back before they come. If you can fix that thing for Heinz there's a chance he'll let us have the villa for a month in August. It's too good an opportunity to miss.'

You're not missing many opportunities, Len thought as he closed the boot lid quietly not to offend her. Everyone in The Rantings knows that you and Heinz are knocking the pictures off the wall in his poncy hairdressing salon every Monday and Friday. He turned to peck her cheek but she was already moving into the house and opening the letters. 'Anything for . . .' he asked plaintively but it was too late. He opened the car door, belted himself in and drove off gratefully past the cretinous postman to the only peace he knew on earth. Sheerpitts Golf Club.

Once parked in the Captain's space, and changed for action, he felt completely recharged; even the grey smudges bruising a clear sky failed to move his smile. He checked in with the competition manager and was told that Aaron was in the bar waiting for their starting time. He joined his opponent, greeted him cordially, chatted over a drink and at precisely 0935 they walked out past the grinning crowd at the big window to the first tee. Normally Len would have turned up early for a practice swing and ten minutes on the putting green, but today was different. However, since he knew he was playing Aaron he had been quite prepared to give the rabbit a couple of holes and halve a few more, taking the match through to the 14th or 15th for decency's sake, and the thought of a 10 and 8 thrashing had not entered his head until Tina had reminded him of the impending visitation of bony Annabel and her revolting Heinz. Christ, it was coming to something when he couldn't even escape from her and her bloody awful friends even at the golf club where he was supposed to be the Captain.

Poor sod, he thought, looking at Aaron as his tee shot stopped rolling before the distant laughter had reached full pitch. Len smashed his like a rocket, straight and long, and together they took the short walk to Aaron's second and third. The little bugger was chanting some kind of weird plainsong, and if the game had been tight Len could have requested him to stop, but it would have been pathetic to do so under present circumstances which, after just under two hours, left the Captain 9 up at the turn. It was working out nicely, apart from the caning his opponent was receiving, but he'd explain it all later, and by good luck he had found one of Archie's bottles by The Grave. He was generously offering first neck to Blomberg when there was a brilliant flash of lightning followed instantly by eye-level thunder. The bottle tingled in his hand and he dropped it in terror. Aaron's Prayers for the Dead assumed a proper relevance and they both instinctively crouched, and looked around anxiously. Everything was cut out by a sheet of rain and the light faded dismally.

When the shock had subsided Len looked at his watch. Still OK for time but not a lot to spare. 'We'll give it a couple of minutes, Mr Blomberg,' he said as they both watched the bottle lying at their feet. After a while the rain eased off but the electric storm intensified; vivid lightning hissed and dried the air till the leaves on the trees crackled. A quarter of an hour went by.

'It's looking much better now,' Len offered. 'Shall we?'

Aaron Blomberg stared at him incredulously. 'Are you crazy, Captain? We'll get killed in that!' He retired back under a sodden Miami straw hat and Len had to agree with him; but Jesus, he was in trouble. He gave it another three minutes.

'Ah, look, Aaron, it's really brightening up over there.' He pointed without much hope towards the USSR but Aaron was adamant and

would not budge. Time was rolling on with the thunder. 'The light's much better. I think we should be getting on.'

His partner was unimpressed. 'It's not the light that kills people. I'm staying here.'

The weather was improving slightly and if the next hole was played quickly Len could call it a day, get back to his hideous guests and avoid another tempest.

'I can't think of a worse place to be in a thunderstorm than a golf course,' Aaron said suddenly. 'These conditions are . . . what do they call it in the rule book?'

Len looked hopelessly at the flickering lightning which was turning his beloved golf course into an old horror film. 'Dangerous to life,' he said dully and then made one last try. 'Look, old chap, please, we can't stand under the trees and there's no point in getting pissed through out here in the open when I need just one more hole and we can call it a day!'

He tailed off, for Aaron had resumed his chanting and was not looking at him. Deliberately, for there was a smile on his face as he heard his Captain speak. Norman Cooper's advice was spot-on. Gurning was 9 up against him and worried! His chanting had worked! The thunder abated but the flashing became more persistent and suddenly it was accompanied by a blaring car horn.

'Oh, shit!' moaned Len as they both looked back to Hinchcliffe's House and saw a car flashing its lights angrily. The noise stopped and a woman burst out of the car, her head covered by a newspaper, but still working the horn. She began to shriek and Len shouted back through the din of Nature and Man. 'I can't, you stupid cow, we haven't finished!'

The distant figure slammed the car door and set off towards them, quickly at first and then, as her heels sank into the soft earth, more slowly but no less sulphurously, Aaron recognized Mrs Tina Gurning as she stabbed her way over the 9th green. The spectre confronted Len, hair and mascara an indistinguishable mess.

'You bastard!' she howled. 'You thoughtless, selfish bastard. They've been waiting at the house for twenty minutes and Heinz is furious. Get in that car!'

She emphasized the invitation by taking her shoe off and throwing it at Len. He ducked and then, with his trolley tucked between his legs, cringed miserably back to the car. Aaron watched in acute embarrassment. Poor man, he thought. But it had to be done. Suddenly he shouted, 'You haven't finished. If you don't finish I'm going to claim the match!'

The figures disappearing in the half-light ignored him. 'Right, Mr and Mrs Gurning. Under the rules I am claiming this match,' he cried.

Aaron was quite taken aback when the lovely Tina turned to him and screamed, 'Claim what you like, fat arse, and go screw yourself while you're at it!'

The weather improved dramatically soon afterwards and Aaron returned to the dressing room, had a shower and, surrounded by grey-faced men, reported to the tournament manager what had elapsed. He was awarded the match, opponent retired, and became the first name to go into the third round of the Vase Knockout Competition.

3

THE MEMBERS AND STAFF

Portraits of some pivotal figures in the merry-go-round that is Sheerpitts.

Sheerpitts Golf Club has 450 members with a waiting list of about the same. Members who actually play and thereby cause a great deal of unnecessary trouble to the Greens Committee number less than 100.

Sheerpitts was the first golf club to realize that the most useless of members was the fanatic who insisted on playing in all weathers instead of getting into position near a drink and spending money where it did the club most good. Damaging the course, using the showers and soap and wearing out towels in no way help the accounts at any club, and at Sheerpitts performance indoors has long superseded virtuosity in the open air. The only accepted oddities in this situation, as ever, are the Scots who play and drink continuously, but their depredations are grudgingly allowed.

The waiting list is not be confused with *The* Waiting List which is a £100 job administered and collected by Ralphie Jukes, President-elect and friend of all who need washing machines, loads of hardcore, tickets of any kind and one-careful-owner cars.

Found abandoned 43 years earlier on an East End building site in London, Ralphie graduated through foster homes, orphanages and pubs to his present position. He quickly learned how essential to life building sites were and also that only fools ever bought anything from shops.

He became a builder and middleman. His houses were of the type which blinded deliriously happy newly-weds who had not previously owned anything more valuable than a bicycle. He offered help with mortgages and prams. Cars were also a possibility, but his great love was buying and selling things he never saw. All his business was conducted on the blower and he simply took money from A for a washing machine and gave some of it to B who knew where one was available. He only dealt with reliable brands and all complaints were to be addressed to the supplier. The small deals were the ones which kept his cutting edge shiny and hard, for he found the big ones easy and automatic and his gipsy heart felt more joy in the sale of a double drainer than in erecting a row of houses. Nevertheless, Jukes Builders (New Town) Ltd was the lever which had eased him into the golf club ten years ago and put him in the position of being the only self-confessed bastard at the bar.

In the Rantings the Masonic Order was almost omnipotent and at Sheerpitts Golf Club it could afford to be benevolent. With The Law (both Wig and Truncheon branches) totally aproned, only a very small group of

non-believers was allowed to follow their curious customs of shaking hands in no particular way and using words of startling banality in introduction. This little crew, with three exceptions, was a spent force destined for ever to sell raffle tickets and turn over hamburgers at the June barbecue if it was raining.

The fact that the three exceptions constituted a group within a group in no way implied respect or admiration for each other. *All* the members, none dissenting, heartily disliked one of them, and avoided him whenever possible. He was the fiery Brigadier, Gerald Patterson, VC, who needed but one drink to tell the world that he lumped Japs and Masons together and that he'd won gongs for killing the little yellow bastards and wouldn't mind sorting out the brotherhood on the same terms.

The fierce ginger-headed dwarf had developed aggressive tendencies from the day at prep school when he had noticed for the first time that his belly button was not in the centre of his body. Whichever way he twisted, it remained slightly to the left, and from that moment on he had determined to take it out on somebody. At first it had been himself and he had battered his way through school, falling out of trees and collapsing rugby scrums at every opportunity. For safety's sake and on medical advice he had been inserted into the Army where his fearlessness and insensitivity rocketed him through the tiers of promotion to become the youngest brigadier in the service at the age of 23, and all this in peacetime.

It was a blessed relief when war broke out and his destructive abilities could be properly directed, but would the Geneva Convention allow him to be unleashed on a people which had given the world Goethe, Nietzsche and Kant? The controversy raged throughout a succession of disasters and defeats in Europe but was resolved by the treacherous actions of the Japanese in the Orient. Their amazing dash through South-East Asia and non-observation of the Convention freed the hands of the War Office and Gerald was sent in all haste to Burma as second-in-command to 'Turngate's Lot'.

This ferocious band of semi-civilized Liverpudlian jungle-dwellers was led by 'Dirty' Turngate, a regular officer despised by his fellows because of strongly held religious beliefs concerning the deleterious effects of washing. At home in the green mansions, his small force harassed the enemy ceaselessly, striking when least expected and melting back under the leafy canopy before any form of retribution could be turned upon them. Their luck lasted for nearly a year until an unexpected and mistaken parachute drop gave away the location of their secret jungle camp to the enemy. They were attacked at dawn by a vastly superior force of crack Imperial Guards and it was at the critical moment when it appeared that they would be overrun that Gerald won his VC, personally accounting for 182 of the attackers with the portable typewriter which had been part of the ill-fated consignment meant for the Chief Clerk, HQ Company, 118th Field Regiment, Royal Artillery, Llewellyn Barracks, Aberystwyth, and dropped in error.

He was brought home, decorated and sedated until further needed, but the atom bomb made him redundant and he left the British Army to seek employment elsewhere. After service in the Foreign Legion and several African private armies, he shipped home and, sticking a pin in a map of the UK, retired on several pensions to Bayonet House, Forced Ranting. Improvements in plastic surgery led him to hope that his stomach's sole feature could be centralized but sadly neither the NHS nor the best that private medicine could offer was remotely good enough to equip his stomach with a symmetrical frontage and he began his retirement in angry isolation.

The Brigadier's only contact with the outside world, apart from occasional calls at The Rest and Be Buggered, was an exchange of letters with his equally violent spinster sister, Courgette, who lived in Scotland. It was she who suggested, in an irritably scrawled and hardly legible missile from Arbroath Cottage Hospital, that he should buy a dog for company. Uncharacteristically, the VC took her advice and Gerald and 'Dirty', the Jack Russell terrier he purchased from Pets 'n' Things, New Town, became inseparable.

The dog savaged every moving object which approached Bayonet House, and this ideal relationship would have endured till death's sting took one of them, had it not ended tragically one morning as the Brigadier took Dirty out and released him for his first maniacal dash of the day. The dog ran to the junction of Sheerpitts Lane and Ranting Old Cut. At the nearby bus stop a Number 7 was commencing the homeward leg of the New Town-Forced Ranting-March Ranting-Forced Ranting-New Town circuit and Dirty leapt on to the vehicle and was gone.

Anxious inquiries at the bus terminal Lost Property Office, the police station and finally in the local press and sub-post office windows elicited no response. The only hint of an answer to the baffling mystery came in an anonymous letter from 'J', a railway porter on Ranting Central who thought he may have seen a dog slipping on to the 09.33 connection to London, but it could have been a labrador, and had the Brigadier considered checking the freezer at the Beijing Lotus Flower Chinese restaurant in Lower Junkin Street?

Steadfastly the distraught owner took up a daily vigil at the fatal bus stop, and an extra service was laid on for pensioners and school outings to view the touching spectacle, but it was only when the South-Eastern Region of the RSPCA asked for permission to erect in his honour a statue on a plinth bearing the inscription 'Semper Fidelis' that he realized that it had been two years, and Dirty was not coming back.

* TRANSLATION: SHINTO! ROOK AT HIS BERRY BUTTON!

Gerald was a man of action and when an even more dreadful prospect loomed, a possible visit from his sister, he made up his mind to *do something*.

Remembering that the local golf club was alive with Masons, whom he had hated since his wartime days but who now might afford a worthwhile target to savage in his retirement years, he applied to become a member at Sheerpitts.

The Committee, despite their suspicion that a name like Patterson might mean yet another Scot in the club, were eventually persuaded by his Beano war record, his background and obvious love of animals.

Almost before they knew it, the lion was in the fold. He joined the drinking set wherever they met on any day at any time, and the Patterson Rush was born. Not him coming in, but them going out.

Three things became immediately apparent to members of Sheerpitts on Gerald's election. Firstly, that he was a golf cheat of Olympic standard, that he utterly hated, loathed and despised the Order of Freemasons and that he was determined never to buy a drink for anyone, even himself, except under the most extenuating circumstances. The first two facts were of no great consequence. The vast majority of members never bothered to swing a club and as his extraordinary holes-in-one were always accomplished alone he was encouraged to continue solo. His violently expressed animosity towards their brotherhood was smiled at and borne with the same maddening tolerance shown by the early Christian martyrs. His mouse roaring at their elephant became a Temple joke, but the relentless stalking at the bar was another thing altogether.

From the first day of his arrival, the previously untroubled and joyful pleasure of strolling in for a session suddenly assumed all the menace and drama of a sundown visit to a Serengeti waterhole. They would nervously sniff the air and search the long grass and there would be nothing, yet the instant the obsequious steward Sidlow placed the drinks in front of a purchaser Gerald would be there in a flurry of, 'How are you? I'll have a large Horse's Neck,' and his victim would be dragged to the ground by his pocket.

The herd at the bar would grab their drinks and wheel away in panic to all corners of the lounge, shivering and watchful as wildebeests until the terror subsided. Gerald struck only once a session and, nursing his plunder, would move amongst them exchanging gossip, criticizing the Masons and telling of his latest hole-in-one.

The initial flood of complaints to the Secretary were met with the famous Hughton smile and outspread hands. Captain Rhino Hughton, RN retd, found enormous satisfaction in telling them that no official move could be made against a man of the Brigadier's record and that the only safe course of action was to be vigilant at all exposed times and run when he appeared.

Safe in his office, Hughton thought it all vastly amusing. He too felt exactly as the little man did about the Masons but a lifetime in the Royal Navy had taught him to be silent on matters not directly concerning him. Most of his service had been under the sea, but his unexpected appointment to the post of Equerry to the Governor-General of the Turks and Caicos Islands had opened his eyes to what he had been missing and he opted for fresh air. The moment he did so he regretted the error.

The closeness and tightness of life in a submarine had accustomed him to accept the shortcomings and noises of his fellow men but not necessarily to love them. Thirty years in very close proximity with 79 others tends to breed a jovial disregard for certain indelicacies which would not pass unremarked at a Buck House garden party, but in Hughton the experience had forged a diamond-hard shell of insensibility which earned him the soubriquet of 'Rhino'.

The Hughton Charm School of Grace and Taste soon became a legend on embassy lawns, and when the aroma of crushed egos and ruptured dignity became overpowering it was suggested to Rhino that he might be better employed in situations where offence would not be taken so easily. Abattoirs and the docks were hinted at, and Rhino left the world of plumed hats and liveried servants for ever. He had no wish to spend the rest of his life climbing up and down ladders so he resigned his commission and swallowed the anchor.

Prospects for an outspoken G and T man, who stood fractionally too near to ladies, and possessed a deafening laugh, were not good but he knew what he wanted and that was half the battle. He needed a berth which was bigger and more private than a submarine but just as water-tight and cleanly run. It only needed a couple of nights poring over Debretts, Burke's and Who's Who to discern the common factor joining those who felt as he did on matters as diverse as contraception and foxhunting. Everyone who was anyone had gone to a good school and belonged to a golf club.

Rhino resolved there and then to inquire further. He would apply to a fairly mediocre golf club situated in pleasant surroundings and there execute the same service he had performed as Captain's secretary on several ships during his naval career and, using the expertise he had acquired in manipulating and insulting people as the Governor-General's equerry, gouge out a cosy niche for himself.

At the Sheerpitts interview he entered the outgoing Secretary's office and Ralphie and Jack Burberry rose to meet him and offer him a drink. The moment the gin and tonic was in his hand Rhino realized with great joy that emptying glasses would be the major part of the inquisition. The President slipped back into his chair and drifted gently away leaving Ralphie and Rhino to go over the fine detail, for the two had spotted kindred spirits at a glance. To Ralphie the Captain was what he imagined himself to be only with the added refinements of a cut-glass accent, service background and a natty line in Gieves blazers. He was smart, insensitive and he knew what he wanted. Ralphie always took to simple unfeeling people like himself and it was obvious to him that in this case the applicant, in exchange for a sheltered nook at Sheerpitts, would be happy to play chief clerk to the Jukes power structure at the club.

Concord was in the air but on the other side of the fence Rhino had spotted Ralphie a mile off. He was lower-deck riff-raff making his way as quickly as possible to the Admiral's cabin by way of the dock gates at midnight. He'd come across many Ralphies in the service and had always avoided them, but this was outside and such driving ambition was just the coat-tail Rhino had been groping for since leaving the Navy. The policies and polemics of Sheerpitts were of no concern to him as long as he was comfortable, safe and had some say in the influence of events. Minutes later Captain Michael Jervis Hughton, RN retd, was officially appointed Secretary of Sheerpitts Golf Club Ltd, and shortly assumed his duties in a brisk and businesslike manner.

He became a new topic of bar chat along with the Brigadier, Wayne Summers, Blomberg, the pig farm, and golf in the shape of the looming Pro-Am. Views and opinions on each subject were expressed forcibly, but it was only later when Marilyn appeared and became the epicentre of the conversation that there was totality in their consensus.

She had arrived at the club as part of the Sidlow family shortly after the new Secretary had demonstrated his power by dismissing the club steward of 25 years for running out of tonic water. Much to its annoyance, Sheerpitts had been forced to advertise the vacancy and amongst the dribble of uninspired replies the one with photographs had so intrigued the committee that an early meeting had been arranged.

Arthur Ransome Sidlow had been selling loft insulation around Milton Keynes and was in an attic when the obscure golfing magazine had caught his eye. Idling through it as he waited for the householder to make him a cup of tea, he saw the club's reserved and pompous plea for a man of impeccable character, and decided there and then to apply. He had run a pub in London for three years before the brewery had caught up with him, but it was only after he had legged it up North and got a job in a working men's club that his eyes were really opened to the sheer criminal ingenuity of simple uneducated men. In no time short measures, and making margarine go a long way, evolved to boxes of this and barrels of that slipping out of the back door to the touching of damp palms. Compared with the broken noses of Lancashire, the idea of a golf club and a host of chinless members attracted him enormously. Endless opportunity in idyllic surroundings and on top of all that a flat and the chance of marrying Marilyn off to someone with money.

At the interview Arthur sealed matters in his favour by producing a snapshot of the family on the nudist beach at San Felipe. Within days the Sidlows had become lock-keepers on the Sheerpitts alimentary canal. Their arrival had provoked a deluge of wide-eyed comment concerning the delectable Marilyn. Only here and there were doubts raised. In the tight

circle that encompassed Margaret Vyner-Kenty, the waspish Ladies'
Captain, the Sidlows were viewed with deep suspicion.

'There'll be trouble,' barked Margaret to her friend Dorothy as she pulled
on her wristband one morning. 'Nude beaches. It's disgusting! I shall watch
the situation very carefully. Right, Dorothy, my honour.'

Captain Margaret's one aim in a spartan life was to drive a golf ball 300
yards. Nothing else mattered. Cooking, cleaning, embroidery – these were
nothing beside the spectacle of a white dot in an azure sky falling away to
bounce to a stop an inch from the flag on a distant green. Orgasmic. All those
exercises with the weights, the tight facial lines and the sweat streaking her
sporting brassière, the panting and gasping . . .

'Margaret, what's wrong?'

'Nothing, Dorothy, nothing. Stand back a little, will you?' She stared
intently at the ball and repeated the litany. Keep the head still and the club
handle passing vertically through the vee of the thumb and first knuckle.
Feet comfortably apart. She remembered her mother saying that fitness was
essential for a young woman's well-being in the world today, even so wasn't
she perhaps overdoing it a little with the weights and enemas? Overdoing it!
That from a woman who collected hub caps. God, how she'd worked to get
to her present state of physical and mental perfection. Concentrate. Move
the hips and pivot on the left foot while drawing the clubhead back and up
with the right elbow tucked in and the left arm straight. Smoothly,
smoothly, and then after a moment's hesitation at the top of the backswing
a swift hard downward pull, smashing through the ball and ending with a
complete followthrough with the head coming up last of all.

'Oh, good shot, Margaret!' Dorothy cried. She shaded her eyes against the
sun and traced the white dot as its arc hunched and faded. The ball fell
gently, silently struck the ground, bounced three times in lazy surprise and
skittered nervously to a halt a cosy nine-iron from the hole. The rattle of the
Lady Captain's driver being savagely rammed back into its bag temporarily
distracted Dorothy's attention and then she looked again at the distant
fluttering yellow square. Once more she turned to her friend. 'That must be
all of 260-270 yards – and from the men's tee!'

Margaret towed her trolley and walked swiftly down the hill, pulling her
visor low to hide the tears of frustration. Thirty yards short! Damn, damn.

'I swear it was almost 300 yards!' Henderson was speaking to the fiercest,
largest ethnic group in the club. He was part of the Scottish clan and they
were gathered in a grim and humourless brown tweed clump by the long
window in the bar. It was their traditional home and an advantageous spot,
giving a fine view of the course and, looking inwards, unrestricted
surveillance of the shadowy bar approaches used by Gerald Patterson.

Henderson was outraged. 'The bloody thing nearly killed me and not a word of apology. That woman is a menace!'

The Highland gathering turned as one to their leader, Doctor Murdo McNish, who drained his glass and glared all around. 'It would never be allowed in Scotland. Dear God, a woman driving off the men's tee!'

Grizzled heads nodded in agreement. English golf clubs and English golfers, with the exception of Archie Gosling, were absolutely useless, McNish went on, as the others, precious amber fluid cradled carefully in their tweedy laps, waited eagerly to join in and condemn without appeal all things English. Bitterly, and sometimes with cause, they would slate the jungle rough, ridiculous flag placings and the Captain's creaky chair. They attacked the lack of parking space and the cruel ring of bunkers protecting the 8th. The English , lounging within earshot, would affect in that infuriating Saxon manner not to hear the monotonous serial as it moved onto lady members and the utter banality of the billiard chalk. The club cat, carpet and curtains, poor cheese and onion sandwiches, tractors on the fairways during play and the steward's perfidy would see them through the daylight hours and, when the packed bar became smokier and more acrid after midnight, they would turn to the vile and disgusting NHS and its spawn who kept them from their beds with their irresponsible nightcalls. This would lead to private patients who never paid their bills on time, and the fool of a Club Secretary who wasted God-knows-how-much money on reminders for the prompt payment of membership fees.

Occasionally they would inject some new contentious titbit into the flux and currently their contempt was aimed at the efforts of Norman Cooper to gild his benefit year by way of strategically placed collecting boxes throughout the club. These had, of course, been ignored with aristocratic indifference for wasn't the fellow making a fortune out of – what's his name? – Blomberg, who must be on his 1000th lesson at least! Good God, was there any justice in an overpaid, underworked golf professional who lazed around in the sun all summer being gifted with the luxury of a benefit year while dedicated honest GPs worked themselves to the grave unnoticed by their patients.

To the remainder of the membership the Scottish mafia were an unspeakable necessity. They gave the club a reason for it to be called a golf club and kept the bar takings on a high throughout the year. They were unavoidably on hand in case of medical emergency and many a slipped disc or ball-strike could recall the parting words of the McNish School of Medicine prior to being driven to Rantings General. 'Come and see me when they've done with you and for God's sake don't have anything to do with Outpatients. Better not come to the surgery, you don't want howling kids and rampant cystitis, pop over to the house. You're in BUPA, aren't you?'

The Celtic fringe watched the evolution of the club and, like many of their English counterparts, marvelled at the antics of Wayne Summers, the assistant pro. More fundamentally, they found it astonishing that a club such as Sheerpitts, with so many glaring faults, should ever have employed an assistant professional in the first place. The reason for his arrival in fact rested with Wayne's superior, Norman Cooper, who had long discovered that hammering the Scotch, being the club professional and avoiding his wife left very little time for teaching golf.

These were pre-Blomberg days and Cooper felt no inclination to stretch himself for the benefit of club members who treated him like grass cuttings. His approach to the previous Secretary regarding the appointment of an assistant professional would have been as disregarded as the seat in the toilet of a Glasgow pub had not Ralphie Jukes intervened. The Vice-President and local builder pointed out that Sunningdale had an assistant pro and that any club that called itself halfway decent had one. If they wanted to stay a second-rate establishment in the eyes of the golfing world, then it was OK with him because he was only a member for the pleasure of the game and their company and it had nothing to do with prestige. But . . . he knew just the lad.

Just the lad was working on one of Ralphie's sites and causing havoc amongst the female wages clerks and taking their minds off the way Mr Jukes liked his books to be fiddled. It meant getting rid of them or him. Ralphie liked them all, but, learning that the lad was keen on sport and knew something about golf, he thought he saw a solution to his problem.

Within a week Ralphie knew that he had struck gold. Wayne Summers was one of those rare people whose effortless brilliance at sport was equally matched by his casual indifference towards it. He was a magnificently built 21-year-old with a blonde classical beauty which even evoked comment from men. Brown as a beach-rat all year round, and radiating friendliness and warmth, he became overnight the darling of the club and second only to Archie Gosling and the Brigadier in the figures he carded.

The members ran out of adjectives to represent his consummate golfing skills. His power, touch and encyclopaedic knowledge of the game in one so young were amazing and it was obvious to anyone who knew one end of a golf bag from the other that here was breathtaking talent. They said that the lustrous child would stay at the club only long enough to solicit sufficient sponsorship to get him to Spain and win the points necessary for European circuit qualification. It was equally plain that with such a battery of skills it was only a matter of time before he was slipping on his Masters green jacket at Augusta.

Patiently Wayne listened to the serious middle-aged men telling him things that he already knew, and he found it hard not to laugh at their

ponderous advice and sombre warnings for he had no intention of doing any of the things they expected of him. Why his blazing charm should be squandered on a game when the dazzling executor of such power could be nuzzling the inside of a silken thigh baffled Wayne. It was unthinkable to a young man who had been playing Doctors since he was 11 that he should go for short grass when there was much more fun to be had in the rough. He could not deny that he enjoyed driving the long 16th with ease, nor that the gasps of his partners were pleasing, but they were not half as stimulating as the sounds uttered by Lt Colonel Beam's German wife Gerta or the enthusiastic groans of Marilyn Sidlow.

Women were first grudgingly admitted to full membership of Sheerpitts Golf Club in 1970, and Wayne had been sent by the gods to make up for the years of shameful discrimination. His great secret and most endearing feature was that he never rested his head on an unwilling bosom, nor was he aggressive, boastful or selective. Using the lovely Marilyn as a datum line and sliding towards the Medusa end of the feminine spectrum, the grimly moustachieod Mrs Protheroe was joyful testimony to his philosophy. Wayne operated only during golf instruction, and well away from the clubhouse, and demonstrated that the fat and ugly and the halt and lame were as much part of his compass as the clear-skinned and sweet-smelling. Success was never taken for granted and on the two legendary occasions when his pupils had stiffened, he had unconcernedly told them to relax – and sure enough the next shot was the best of the day.

Tales of Wayne found their way by some strange osmosis back to the Ladies' locker-room, and thence throughout the club and even as far as USAAF Miles Ranting, where Wayne became a risqué logo on several high-performance aircraft. From then on his activities fell into the Worst Kept Secrets of the War category, openly spoken of but completely missed by those seeking to find out the facts. Every lady concerned knew quite clearly and definitely what was going on between the Stud and Mrs/Ms Z but firmly believed that her own particular liaison with Wayne was safely wrapped in an impenetrable cloak of darkness. Each happy recipient would breathlessly agree with the donor that this had been a one-off, and that it must never NEVER happen again or it would wreck their marriage and cost him his job. It did happen again, it saved their marriages and he was still driving 350 yards at Sheerpitts. Two refusals in as many years left him with a strong credit balance and those who surrendered to his ardour enjoyed the union to its fullest.

The successes of the young assistant professional tickled the gentry at the bar for no man believed for a moment that he was the husband of the red nails currently raking Wayne's nut-brown back. 'I don't know where the bugger gets the energy from. Archie Gosling just told me that someone told him that they saw Wayne and Mavis Fulbright going at it like a sewing machine. Back of the dog-leg 7th, it was.' 'Really. I heard it was Tim Sage's old lady!' The speakers would then stare at each other over their drinks, certain in the knowledge that the lady referred to was in actual fact the other man's wife. Further embarrassed silence would be cut short by the wild panic of the Patterson Rush Phenomenon and, by the time the two met up with each other again, events and Wayne had passed them by.

4

THE COURSE

Descriptions of each hole by Norman Cooper, the professional, after a row with his wife, Edna.

Described in the *Sheerpitts Guide* (Jukes the Printer, £2.50) as the ideal professional, ruddy-faced Yorkshireman Norman Cooper has been teaching club members for nearly three decades. This year, his benefit season, is his last and so we are only just in time to plunder his vast experience.

It is a fine clear morning with hardly any wind, the ground is dry and the greens are lightning fast. Moorcroft the greenkeeper has left the rough for two weeks and it is certainly tacky. Near his hut it is especially tacky with the remnants of endless cups of tea which Moorcroft brews and consumes throughout the day. The fairways, however, are pure velvet and there is a blue sky to steeple your drive into. Let's wait on the 1st tee for a moment and allow Norman to finish his second large one of the day. Here he comes, so why not jump up on his chunkily aggressive shoulder and eavesdrop on him as he plays his annual solo round to see if the magic is still there. He knows Sheerpitts better than anyone except old Moorcroft, though the relationship between the two is much the same as the union between himself and Edna Cooper, his wife and burden for 38 years.

The morning had started with a flaming row and Norman had stormed out of the pro's shop leaving Edna sitting behind the counter storing up thunder for a second encounter. Like many men, Norman finds the fresh and open air precious when the old lady is on the rampage and he can take his spite out of the little white pill on the long 5th. His trolley crunches over the gravel and then its sound is stifled by grass. Norman reaches the 1st tee and expertly removes the wrapping from a glistening new 'Norman Cooper 666'. Here we go.

Hole 1. The Bus Stop. 363 yards. Par 4.
'I don't know what's the matter with that bloody woman! I can do without that kind of hassle first thing in the morning. Menopause! Nobody ever stops to think what men go through during the bloody thing. What with her face and that miserable lot of tight-arsed bastards in there. Right, I'll show them a bloody thing or two . . .

Yes. Now. Pull out the trusty old driver, give it a quick twiddle, a few grossly exaggerated practice swings to show those pillocks in there who's on top of his job, thank you very much, and here we go.

Right. We need a longish straight drive because we've got the trees all along the left side of the fairway hiding the course and clubhouse from

Sheerpitts Lane and the poor people, and more trees on the right. The fairway looks flat but in actual fact there's an invisible gulley 200 yards from the tee running across it. The trick is to finish this side of it just on the upslope, giving you a 9-iron to the smallish green which slopes to the right. Anyway, I think it slopes to the right. I shouldn't have had two stiff ones so early, but God! she gets up my nose at that time of day. Right, these two kidney bunkers are on either side of the approach to the green, and with the flag in the top half it's essential to place the ball downhill because it's safer putting uphill. It's safer not getting married but we still do it. By gum, if it wasn't for that Jewish feller I'd beat meself to death with a cleek. When all else goes wrong there's always the Blomberg Pension Plan to see me through. With a bit of luck there must be at least another 200 lessons there before he finally calls it a day and he doesn't look the sort to give in easily.

Oh, bugger it! The slope's to the left after all. Another three-putter. Well, there you are, you see! It may look like a simple shortish hole, but if you don't concentrate properly you get a five!

Hole 2. Monks A'Ranting. 334 yards. Par 4

This one is a sod. You've got to belt it over a line of trees which run right across the fairway at 165 yards, then go for a pitch to the green which is level but partly hidden by the trees. Behind the green there is is a crescent of young saplings and behind them you've got the brook, so you can see why I don't like this one. It's named after the beer made in these parts for hundreds of years which, personally, coming from Yorkshire, I think tastes like cat's piss.

I'm going for a lofted drive, say a 3-wood, over the trees and then a nice pitch hoping I'll stop on the green which is level and unprotected by bunkers.

Oh, shit! I omitted to mention the two traps on the right of the fairway and short of the green. Another five. Ten shots and sixteen to play. Be lucky to beat 86. Bloody bitch! Why can't she keep her mouth shut till after breakfast.

Hole 3. The Führer Bunker. 156 yards. Par 3.

Here we are at the first short hole on the course, occasionally known as The Kick in the Arse. As the name implies the two huge bunkers protecting the pin are old bomb craters from the war and were the result of a Dornier trying to escape from a Spitfire and jettisoning its bombs before crashing on Adams's pig farm. Why the silly bugger didn't bomb the clubhouse *and* the pig farm no-one will ever know but I suppose he had other things on his mind at the time.

I use a 6- or 7-iron, depending on the wind which blows across the line, and try to ignore Sheerpitts Brook which is 60 yards from the tee. The

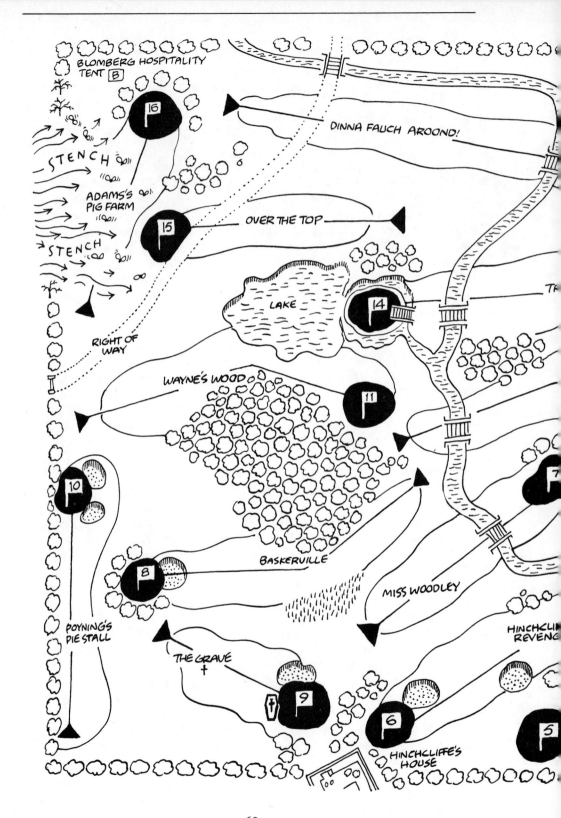

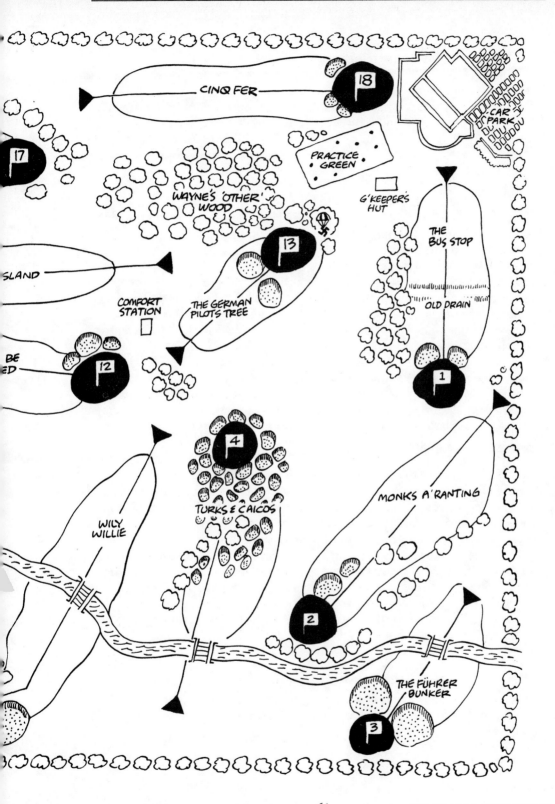

bunker on the right is the Führer and the left one is the Kick.

The green is totally dwarfed by both traps which must be 30 feet deep and 200 feet in circumferance. At no part can you play out towards the green, and the only sensible course of action is to play short of the bunker or walk back to the clubhouse and have a Scotch. I've played a few courses in my time but even at Birkdale they don't need a pothole rescue team. You earn your three here, except the Brigadier who claims to have done it in one, three times. Lying little bugger.

Hole 4. The Turks and Caicos. 373 yards. Par 4.

This is a perfectly ordinary dog-leg to the left after you've teed off over the brook. When you're congratulating yourself on finishing in a perfect position just to the right of the clump of oak trees which mask the elevated green, you suddenly notice that there must be nine or ten traps of various sizes completely encircling the flag. In actual fact there are 37 bunkers of varying dimensions on the hole, which is called the Turks and Caicos because from the air it looks like that chain of Caribbean islands, or so Surgeon-Commander Repton told his fellow members in the late Twenties, and they believed him.

After the dog-leg it's just a case of having the bottle to stick the ball as high in the air as you can for a dead stop. There's no way of running on to the green without going into a trap. On the other hand, if you think you can guide your ball through the 18 inches which is the maximum space between any of the bunkers, good luck to you because that puts you in the Archie Gosling class. I wonder if my dear wife has cooled down yet.

Hole 5. Wily Willie. 502 yards. Par 5.

Here you come to your first big test. By now Archie would be on his third bottle. Big hitters should watch out that they don't drop in the brook which crosses the fairway 250 yards from the tee. Better to lay up from the tee because the ground in front of the brook is flat and safe.

From there, five trees on your right, 200 yards ahead, hide the green (and one of Archie's bottles) and turn the second half of this hole into a dog-leg, so a 3-iron with a bit of luck should see you sitting between the trees and the big pot bunker to the left of the green, which is on a high plateau with a slope to the left. The green itself is about as big as Wembley Stadium and after your lovely approach shot stops on or near it you think you're home and dry. That's when you three-putt.

Hole 6. Hinchcliffe's Revenge. 370 yards. Par 4.

You'll love this one. The hole itself is a perfectly simple straight belt with a driver, a pitch to the green followed by a roll-in with the putter. The only

Bones Attract Mammoth Interest

Bones discovered recently about 30 feet down in a local sand and gravel quarry are the centre of a fierce row between the site owner, Mr Ralph Jukes, and The Rantings County Museums and Arts officer Dr Eric Dufton.

Immense interest has focussed on the remains since they were uncovered during excavation work two weeks ago. Dr Dufton, a Mammoth expert, is seeking Department of Environment support for a suspension of work in the quarry until a detailed investigation of the site has been carried out.

'It would mean sifting through every inch of ground material,' he told me, 'because soil sticking to the bones could well contain seeds, insects and leaves. Eventually all the evidence could be pieced together to provide a picture of conditions existing 10,000 to 40,000 years ago. I am confident that the remainder of the bones are still there and that we will end up with almost a complete Mammoth.'

The site owner, local businessman Mr Ralph Jukes, said that he sympathized with Dr Dufton but any suspension of work in the quarry would seriously affect local employment prospects. He agreed that the bones were of great scientific and public interest and was prepared to allow visitors into the site to view the bones from a safe observation platform, for a small admission fee.

'Museums charge people to come in,' he said, 'so I am only falling into line with current practice. I am a keen environmentalist

The man who started it all, Samson Ketch, points to the bones of contention.

'I was driving the big excavator when suddenly I saw these white things in the ground. At first I thought they were German bombs and this is exactly how I found them. Man, they haven't been touched since the Mammoth just fell down a million years ago! It was really exciting and me and Caresse are now into Palaeontology and things.'

Mr Ketch is pictured with his girlfriend, Miss Caresse Pringle, speaking to archaeologists on the Mammoth site.

and part of the proceeds will be donated to Friends of the Earth. We hope to open in a day or two and the public may use our hamburger hut, play-area and toilets.'

A government spokesman said that Dr Dufton's request was being considered, but the local DHSS work-load and costs always had to come first in an area like The Rantings with its higher-than-average unemployment figures.

dangers are a small bunker to the left of the fairway, at 180 yards, and another one, even smaller, situated to the right of the green and the big house looking at you from behind the flag. This was Sam Hinchcliffe's house, and the moment you start thinking about him you see hidden perils in the green and you're kettled.

You will have read earlier how old Sam took his revenge on the club by ordering his butler to rip up the green by dead of night with a JCB. Totally wrecked it. Afterwards the club considered moving the green, but since that would have meant giving in to a coarse Northerner they spent thousands on putting it right. It looks flat enough but the instant you start thinking about what happened on that dark night, your nerve goes along with your par.

Hole 7. Miss Woodley. 344 yards. Par 4.

I've no idea why it's called that. I've asked everyone connected with the place and nobody knows. I can only think that perhaps the founder was guilty of an indiscretion with someone before he lost his leg in the First War, or it could even have been the stage-name of the nun who looked after him in France.

Drive straight and hard. I know it's easy to say this, but if you play Sheerpitts the obvious way, she'll be kind to you like Miss Woodley. Your second shot is the killer. Underhit and you're in the brook. Push the bugger through and you're in a crescent of trees behind the long narrow green.

Hole 8. Baskerville. 452 yards. Par 4.

This is the most savage dog-leg on the course, hence its obvious name. The line to take is down the fringe of Wayne's Wood and keeping clear of a large patch of Ranting grass rough on the left which is a bugger to escape from. Ideally your drive should leave you with a clear view of the pin 250 yards ahead.

If your second shot is short you'll find your approach to the green compromised by a sand trap directly in front of the flag, while behind the putting surface a half-moon of trees is waiting for you. It's best if your second shot trends to the right of the hole. The green is fairly small and level so don't be too ambitious. If you do find yourself in the trap all is not lost. Archie Gosling has been known to keep a bottle of amber liquid just under the near lip, so I might allow my second to drift a little south of the equator.

Hole 9. The Grave. 301 yards. Par 4

According to the little plaque on the green there are 108 grinning skulls under the bunker floor, laughing at you as the ball keeps rolling back between your toes. When the course was built, the Colonel only employed one-legged men for the job and every Long John in the country came piling up here for the work. He had to turn a lot down and when it came to the final selection those who had nearly made it and didn't couldn't face returning to the dole and started tucking into the mushrooms which still grow in Wayne's Wood. Those horrible redcap things with white spots. The silly pillocks were all found as stiff as boards early the following day and the old man, who was as daft as a brush, fixed it with the coroner and the vicar to consecrate the new bunker and plant the deceased under it.

What you've got now is a decent hole ruined, because if you aim for the flag you hit the bloody plaque and bounce into the bunker, and who likes treading on people's heads? On top of that you can see Hinchcliffe's house through the trees, so all in all this hole is one you could well do without.

Anyway, you've done your worst and there's the first nine under your belt. If you've scored 34 to 36 you're a better man than I am, Gunga Din, or a cheat like the Brigadier.

Hole 10. Poyning's Pie Stall. 343 yards. Par 4.

This one is named after the Fat Boy of Lower Ranting. Apparently the line of trees which make up the western boundary of the course was once the site of the old Sheerpitts Fayre, with fire eaters, ferret jugglers and all that mediaeval stuff. To help wash down the Monks ale there used to be a famous pie-stall, and that's where fat Algy liked to demonstrate his prodigious eating feats. Frankly I don't believe that anyone could put away 36 dozen meat pies at one go, but that's what they say he did. Bloody hell, talk about £400 a ton for your droppings!

They still make Poyning's Pies in the New Town, but they're all crust and I've eaten better tortoises. The hole itself is fairly gentle and all you have to do is run up alongside the trees and play always to the left of the flag. That way you can ignore the bunkers at 5 and 1 o'clock to the pin and go in by the side door.

Hole 11. Wayne's Wood. 339 yards. Par 4.

The most famous hole on Sheerpitts golf course and the source of endless pleasure, amusement, scandal, gossip and total exhaustion. It's the part of the course where my assistant professional, the insatiable Wayne, exercises that part of his body which, if it were tattooed, would spell out 'SITS' one minute and 'SHEERPITTS' the next. He never gets tired and to be honest I've not heard a female member complain.

His great secret is that, like all the great lovers, he doesn't care who or how. There isn't a feller in the club who wouldn't eat his kids for a crack at Marilyn Sidlow, but Wayne gets away with it because he services the bangers as well as the sports cars. He does it with such style, what's more, that no husband would ever dream that his trouble-and-strife is wearing a contented smile for any other reason than it's good drying weather.

I did hear that the Lady Captain turned him down. However, he must be dedicated to even try it with that vinegar bottle, but that's his great strength. He doesn't discriminate, nor does he go where he is not welcome. First creak of disapproval from a sporting bra and suddenly it's a golf lesson, the next shot is invariably the best of the day and all is forgiven.

~DEBIT~

As for the hole itself, its only defence is Sheerpitts Lake which spills onto the left side of the fairway. Keep your drive just clear of Wayne's Wood on the right, stopping short of the lake, and then hit your second shot up to the pin. Quite often you can't see the whole green thanks to the trees which throw a misleading shadow over it, so it's traditional just to stand there and complain bitterly about the idiot who designed the hole. This doesn't help your approach but it does give Wayne and his companion time to make their excuses and leave.

Hole 12. Rest and Be Buggered. 416 yards. Par 4.

This is the last time for some time that you will be travelling away from Adams's pig farm, so when you get to the distant green take a breather in the little Comfort Station. There are trees to your left and parallel with them a big bunker for the slice. The green is defenceless to the right and that's the way to pick up your par. Mark your card, say a little prayer and rest, for soon you will be entering the world of that swine Adams and his horrible piggery. You will look back on the 12th in a few short minutes and remember it as nothing but a mirage.

Comfort Station! That's the bloody Yanks for you!

Hole 13. The German Pilot's Tree. 145 yards. Par 3.

The famous tree itself is the tallest of a group of beeches behind the green, which is protected at the front by two bunkers which make a nice little triangle with the flag. The whole thing looks a doddle. Hit a 5-iron as close to the pin as you can and be down in a couple of putts. Don't you believe it! If you thought the 6th green was bad, take a look at this one and try not to feel seasick. It's got ridges like a corrugated tin roof. Take it from me, there's only one way in, and that's in a direct line between the tee and the green. Simple when you know how, but some members haven't rumbled it in forty years and I'm buggered if I'm telling them.

Hole 14. Treasure Island. 528 yards. Par 5.

This is a long one with no problems for the first 450 yards, so just get into the ball and enjoy yourself. Hard hitters have a definite advantage and you'll have to grin and bear it as the animals drive miles ahead of you. The Lady Captain loves to humiliate me on this hole but I always get my own back on the green because she can't swim.

I have never seen a flag so well protected by water. The brook running across the front of the green is bad enough, but it's only when you're trembling over what club to take for your approach to the pin that you realize that there's more. A tributary runs towards the green and fills the

moat which surrounds the flag almost completely. Behind the green is Sheerpitts Lake so bring your wellies.

I always play safe and attack the hole from the right. Trees are a hazard but if you're not sure about your pitching, and you haven't got a life jacket, this is the only dry road. The 'Treasure', incidentally, is Archie's and he usually leaves it in the moat to keep cool. You'll be happy to walk away from this hole without squelching – even if it does mean you are now at the gates of Hell.

Hole 15. Over the Top. 207 yards. Par 3.

Now is the moment when you wonder whether the man who invented bacon sandwiches was an agent of the Devil. Adams's Pig Farm is directly ahead of you, and the realization that the 16th compels you to play along the entire frontage of the place, is as full of pleasurable anticipation as Athlete's Foot. The only advice I am prepared to offer as a professional golfer and fellow human being is hit the thing and hole it as quickly as possible. I have no idea how the green plays because, like everyone else, I pass this part of Sheerpitts in haste. One final word of warning. The flag may be missing. Flags in the atmosphere surrounding the pig farm last about two weeks.

Hole 16. Adams's Pig Farm 312 yards. Par 4

The piggery runs along the left side of the hole, but not as fast as the golfers who race along the far side of the fairway. A ragged line of trees guards the back of the putting area from 9 to 3 o'clock, and apart from these the 16th has no ground hazards of any kind. Par four for such an unprotected hole may seem overgenerous to a visitor used to breathing the atmosphere of Mercury or Jupiter, but it should be remembered that it is much harder to hit a moving golf ball than a stationary one, which is what the waves of stench make necessary here. The record from tee to rattle of ball in cup is currently held by 'Twitchy' Pomfrett, who from a standing start in 1976 completed the distance in 2 minutes 14.83 seconds, and apart from his tee shot at no time stood motionless. 'A remarkable performance,' said the President in his speech at the AGM, 'from a man who normally agonized for so long over a putt that birds reared their young in his bag.'

The reeking Adams never moves off the farm, but occasionally comes out to eff and blind at passing golfers. The local tradesmen leave all provisions and communications of any kind at a point 900 yards upwind from the farm.

But why am I spending so much time on this hole when I have no intention of playing it? Let's just get the hell out of it and run to the 17th tee.

Hole 17. Dinna Fauch Aroond. 541 yards. Par 5.

If there's one thing I hate more than women on a golf course it's the twee little Scottish names they dream up for certain holes. 'Jockie's Burn', 'Deil's

Creel', 'Wullie's Brawest', 'Dun Whinny' and that sort of stuff. I've tried my best to stop them doing it here but Sheerpitts, like every golf club in the land, is infested with Jocks.

Scotland versus the Rest of the World is without doubt my worst day of the year. The little hairy men always seem to win and they've quietly taken over the club in the last few years. Well, not completely, not with Ralphie's hot little hands dipping into all the pies, but they still have more influence than their numbers deserve. It's the bloody doctor business. We've got 17 poison dwarfs in the club and 15 are in the cough-and-spit trade, of which 12 are on the brink of cyrrhosis so I suppose it's not all bad news. It was McNish who came up with the name for the escape from Adams's Pig Farm, and when he suggested it at the bar one day, all the pompous old farts on the various committees said, 'Oh, I say, what a capital name.' Nobody except the Jocks has any idea what it's supposed to mean, but when was there any justice in golf club politics?

As for playing the hole, Sheerpitts Brook runs parallel to the fairway which is open on both sides, and the hazards come late and nasty. The brook suddenly whips across plumb in front of the green and the bridge complicates matters further, but if you can beat the water the putting area is flat and fast. The only additional point to remember is that Wayne's Other Wood stands erect and passionate behind the green, so a good loud cough or cry of relief is expected.

Hole 18. Cinq Fer. 353 yards. Par 4.

More foreign names, but at least it isn't Glaswegian. The home hole calls for a straight drive because it is a very narrow fairway with Wayne's Other Wood on the right and the boundary trees on the left. At 200 yards the ground falls away sharply to the right, so underhit to stay short and give your second a chance, otherwise you will be faced by The Testicles, two adjacent sandpits which guard the flag on the right. The trap on the left of the green slims down your approach even more, but if you've got this far – go for it! The clubhouse soaks will be giving you the evil eye as usual, but I find a cheery wave often has them turning away in disgust so you might like to try that.

I gave up scoring after the outward half, but it was a reasonable round considering that I didn't play the 16th. Ah well, perhaps a couple of quickies in the groundsman's hut and then back to the lovely Edna. Mind you don't walk too fast on the way in. The final 100 yards is called Coronary Hill. We've had a couple of infarcts and a fatality here over the last couple of years, and one chap ruined a good eagle by popping his clogs through too much haste. We don't want more business for McNish & Co!'

Blomberg's Progress

Aaron Blomberg stood in the Sheerpitts Hall of Fame. Around him, proud and shining, were the cups, goblets, putters and shields won and lost by the membership over the years. Blomberg searched the rolls of honour, as he had done many times before, but Cohens and Rabinowitzes were there none. This was going to change. With £800 of new clubs and victory in the first two rounds of the Vase under his belt, who could stop a new name being etched in gold on the creamy oaken board up there on the wall. He looked down at the superbly cut McGregor tartan trousers which his best craftsmen had made for him to wear for the Vase competition, and laughed like Errol Flynn.

Who could stop him now?

5

THE PRO-AM CHARITY GOLF TOURNAMENT

The Tournament Committee bites off more than it can chew, and finds that the centre is Japanese-flavoured.

Ralphie Jukes sat in his Portakabin office on the Dream Rantings building site. Looking out the filthy window, he watched the brickies and the plasterers vie with the plumbers and tilers for total immobility and laughed.

How different it would be after lunch when they were all fresh from the Rest and Be Buggered, going up and down the ladders like yoyos without a care for safety. By half-past three they'd be casually flicking dog-ends from the rooftops with unerring accuracy into the stagnant puddles amongst the rubble and grinning at the wide-eyed first-time buyers as they pointed to imagined sitings for their fridges and three-piece treasures. Then they'd climb back into their cars and drive to the Rantings Building Society where Mr Alfred Fisher would have the forms waiting for their signature.

Ralphie leaned back nursing his mug. The weather hadn't been too bad and not too much time had been lost to rain and industrial disputes. On top of that he'd managed to save a bit on windows by not installing any in the bathrooms on Dream Rantings Estate. Illumination came from a fancy new Italian lighting system which hugged the wall and also gave off heat. He'd picked it up cheap via Colonel Ooks from somewhere in Morocco in exchange for 20,000 videos saved for him by business associates from the pyromaniacs at HM Customs. If the new owners wanted a window in the bathroom it was OK with him, and Mr Fisher would add it to the mortgage, but why would anyone want a window-cleaner looking at his wife in the bath?

The telephone did its bird impression and Ralphie looked through to the outer office for Doreen, the girl who saw to it that his mug became dirtier each day. No sign. Playing football with the chippies as usual. He rose with a grunt of annoyance to answer its irresistible mating call. He hated to be the first to pick up a telephone and let it ring a little longer. Where the hell was she? The instrument refused to give up hope and he reached across and picked it up.

'Hello?'

'Is that Mr Ralph Jukes?' asked a dimly familiar voice.

'Who wants to know?' replied Ralphie with his habitual caution.

'This is Terry Wogan speaking. So you want me to come to your golf tournament, do you . . .'

SECOND TOURNAMENT COMMITTEE MEETING

Ralphie Jukes, Tournament Director, carefully scrutinized his fellow committee members as he pretended to shuffle the agenda papers in front of him. Secretary Hughton and three dummies, that was the score – just what he wanted so he could run the thing his way. Facing him, and at the opposite end of the oak table, Rhino Hughton smiled back without emotion and, yawning expansively, folded his hands across the back of his head. On Ralphie's immediate left the accountant Stanley Mountford, neatly arranged his correspondence on an open folder. On his left hand sat Ian Fletcher, the Rantings' most prominent architect and designer of the glassless refrigerated bus shelters on the Orbital Road. He was staring out of the window to a far-off mountain top on which stood a fairy-tale golf clubhouse made entirely of spun gold reinforced polystyrene and fibreglass sheeting. Facing him but taking no notice was Robert Snodin, manager of the Hinchcliffe Plaza branch of Benskins Bank, tapping happily at his pocket calculator with a blunt finger. The Tournament Director was interested to see what his dummies had accomplished over the last few days, and called the meeting to order.

'Right, gentlemen, this is our second meeting and if the Secretary will take notes perhaps we can thunder into action. Do we need any refreshments? Perhaps when we've finished. Good. Now, it was agreed that we make various inquiries into the setting up of a really first-class, high quality Pro-Am charity tournament and that tasks be allotted to members of the committee along those lines. Can we start with you, Stan?'

Mountford adjusted his thick-lensed bifocals and placed his hands evenly distanced across the folder. When people asked Stanley why all accountants were dull he would reply, 'Why not?' He was cosy and safe and knew of no other socks than grey. He stared slowly around the table and reported thus:

'Gentlemen, I have, as you know, received a reply from the PGA, Southern Region. This lays out the general requirements necessary for them to endorse such a tournament as we hope to stage. It boils down to this. Firstly, £5,000 prize-money for their professionals. This is apportioned out as £750 first prize and diminishing in proportion down to 5th place. The PGA will take 2½% of the prize money deducted at source from each professional's cheque. There can be additional prizes such as a car for a hole-in-one at a specified hole, and where holes are sponsored by firms or companies, products of those firms or companies to the retail value of and not more than £110 may be given as prizes to amateur players. Amateurs and celebrities usually are awarded prizes such as cut-glass, decanters, trays, etc. On our acceptance of these conditions they will circulate their members and provide us with 30 professional golfers. I have made copies of their letter for you to study in detail and . . .'

'What kind of 30 professional golfers?' Ralphie broke in suspiciously. 'Blimey, if the top whack is £750 we're not going to get any big names!'

'I telephoned them on receipt of this letter with exactly that point in mind,' replied Mountford. 'Of the men they can offer, few will be involved in any major tournaments this year, and to be brutally frank I got the impression that most of them are over the top. On the other hand it was pointed out to me that the figure of £750 was a suggested one and there was nothing to stop us increasing it to something more attractive. I am not offering opinions, only facts, but I must say that unless we do somehow manage to bolster up the inducements the only television golfers we'll recognize will be from black-and-white days.'

There was an air of disappointment around the group, and Ralphie forced himself upright. 'Well, that's not a very good start, is it. We won't get sponsorship if they can't do better than that. We want top names to go with our big celebrities!'

Mountford smiled. 'Where will the money come from? You won't attract the players without it, but the sponsors won't cough up unless you give them well-known faces.' He paused. 'The only solution that I can see to the problem is Shin Hai Zips. Perhaps the Tournament Director can tell us if the rumour about them coming to the Rantings is true?'

Ralphie twitched in his chair. Apart from Sir Harold Wing, the ineffably corrupt and ambitious MP for The Rantings, who had confided the news to him, he thought it was still a closely guarded secret that the Japanese planned to invade the area. He coughed. 'Well, er, this is pretty confidential but . . . yes, there is a strong possibility that they will be opening a huge factory in the New Town area.'

'Then there's your answer!' Snodin said, looking up from his calculator. 'They'll be getting big government tax concessions and all sorts of long-term low-interest loans to cut the unemployment figures in this region. They'll have money to burn.'

There was a chain reaction of nodding and Ralphie turned to Snodin. 'Robert!'

The banker flicked his calculator off with a stubby finger and leaned forward on his elbows. 'Well, there has been a lot of vague talk about Shin Hai Zips coming here and let's hope it's true. It certainly alters the scenario I have prepared. I envisaged a formula which should provide, after expenses, a profit of around £10,500. That is of course working on the original figure of £5,000 for the PGA. Our first task will be to sell each hole to sponsors. At £1,000 per hole we have £18,000 in the kitty straight off. For his money the sponsor is entitled to three amateur places in the Pro-Am, free buffet meals and an advertisement gratis in the souvenir programme. He will also be allowed to erect a hospitality tent or marquee near the hole he is sponsoring to entertain and water his guests. Catering is the problem. If everything turns out as we want it to and we have a fine day, I can see maybe two or three thousand people out there on the course and heaven knows how many in the clubhouse. I suggest Sidlow does the VIP food and we call in Trunions or some other outside caterers . . .'

Ralphie could see golden vistas opening. 'Leave that to me, Robert. I think I know just the people . . .' He wrote rapidly on his pad. 'Go on, what were you saying?'

Snodin continued. 'I will contact as many local firms and companies as I can and offer them the opportunity to sponsor a hole or even a half-hole depending on the response. If it's not so hot a reaction perhaps I'll go direct to Shin Hai and . . .

'That's alright, Robert, I'll attend to Shin Hai. You can leave that to me. Right, that's the setting up and sponsoring reviewed with several courses of action open to us. Let me give it some thought. What's next in the agenda? Oh, bugger! It's Security. For God's sake don't mention anything about private security firms to Ken Dowty. He'll go bananas. We'll let him think we're using his lads if he asks, but I know a chap who runs a very tight little outfit with a flawless record. Right. Next. Tents and stands. That's your baby, Ian. Got any ideas?'

Fletcher sat erect and gently grasped handfuls of air. 'I see the marquees, green and white stripes, in a sweeping crescent around the clubhouse with the large central presentation area on a raised dais overlooked by scaffold stands . . .'

Ralphie smiled and broke in. 'Ian, don't think I'm stepping on your toes but I have some good connections in your field. If you can come up with a better deal than I get we'll buy it, but just give me first go, will you.' He turned to the pad again as he went on talking. 'You lay the whole lot out, Ian, you've got a very nice touch. Ah! We've forgotten the souvenir programme!'

'What about Jukes the Printers?' Hughton suggested, looking at the ceiling.

Ralphie glared at him. 'That's a good idea. I could produce a good colour one at a favourable price . . . no, for gratis as it's a charity. I'll make a note.' He wrote briefly and looked up again. 'We haven't done too badly for a short meeting, have we. Is there anything else before we get to the bar?'

His leaving gesture was arrested by Hughton. 'Dr McNish buttonholed me yesterday. He was concerned about the professionals' reaction to our course. He's worried that they'll eat it up as it is at the moment and he wants the tee markers pulled back and pin placement to be as difficult as possible. I don't know what you think . . .'

Ralphie scribbled on his pad. 'That's a nasty one and I'll get some advice from the Greens' Committee. McDonald, I think. Have a word with Jock about that, Captain Hughton, will you, and report back at the next get-together. Anything else? No, right, I think that's about all we can handle at the moment, chaps, so before I ask you to look at your diaries and tell me if the 16th is OK for our next gathering I'd like you, Stan, to find out about Pluvius insurance . . .'

Gently Ralphie spread the load – starting times, car parking, rubbish disposal, etc. – and after nods and thank yous closed the meeting with a promise to convene again on the 16th. All rose gratefully and, after opening the TV lounge door quietly and seeing no sign of the Brigadier, headed for the bar.

FINAL MEETING OF THE PRO-AM
CHARITY TOURNAMENT COMMITTEE

The Committee sat at the table looking at their alien. What was happening to the world? First it was Jews and now *this*!

The Japanese visitor smiled, and apart from his expensive suit and flawless skin seemed alarmingly at home in the TV lounge of an English

Sex Change on Rates Row

by Steve Poynter

A sex-change Councillor is at the centre of a dispute involving £3,000 of Bishop's Ranting New Town ratepayers' money.

Left-wing Councillor Dolly Pringle was elected to South Hinchcliffe Council in February of this year and was formerly brewery employee Wilf Moult. It is alleged that she had her sex change thanks to a loan from the Ranting Workers Cooperative and Tenants League, where she was a part-time worker. The RWC&TL has since been wound up and the Hinchcliffe Plaza Flat Dwellers Federation claims that the debt has been passed on to them and they want the money back.

Plaza Chairman Frank Allright said, 'The money is ours and at the last meeting there was an overwhelming vote that she should pay it back. Why should the ratepayers foot the bill for a private operation which was performed purely to draw attention to another matter?'

A spokesman for the defunct RWC said that Miss Pringle had originally borrowed £1,500 but the operation had 'gone wrong' and that a further £1,500 had been given to 'put things right'. Countering for Ranting Young Conservatives, Mr Tim Burberry said that the Labour Party would go to any lengths to protect their own and that the sole purpose of the dispute was to attract publicity to a small group campaigning for the release of a local man from prison.

Mr Burberry was prepared to produce evidence that brewery worker Wilf Moult had his employment terminated when it was found that he had recently had a sex-change operation and was now Miss Dolly Pringle.

Miss Pringle was not available for comment but her father, Mr Walter Pringle, denied the allegations and said, 'Our Doll is so confused, she don't know whether to stand up or sit down!'

golf club. Ralphie shifted in his chair to break the spell.

'Right, everyone, first let me introduce the Deputy Managing Director of Shin Hai Zips, Mr . . . er . . . Nobusuke Kinichiwa. He's here informally to see how we're organizing the Pro-Am, and to offer any suggestions from his, er, company's point of view. May I say what a pleasure it is to see you here, Mr Kinichiwa.'

'Kinichiwa!' said the sallow intruder, pronouncing his name correctly. To their surprise and horror he did not rise and bow humbly but gave each Committee member the merest flicker of a nod. His hosts clumsily returned the welcome, each thinking, 'The little bastard thinks he's running the show already! We'll see about that, Mr Chickenwire, oh yes!'

Ralphie went on. 'I thought it would be the ideal moment for us to get to know each other.' The sweat was still trickling down his armpits after his guest's near-miss with the fiery Brigadier. The tiny war hero had become gruesomely attentive to the flood of radio and press comment on Shin Hai's impending arrival in the Rantings and was now in a high state of readiness. Aware of this, Ralphie and Hughton had laid careful plans for the reception of Mr Kinichiwa. Together they had combed the lane and car park for any sign of Patterson and had left an unattended drink on the bar as a diversion. So far so good, but when the Nissan rolled up, to Ralphie's surprise Kinichiwa stepped out of the car accompanied by Sir Harold Wing! The MP had glared at Ralphie when, instead of being ushered in through the veneered front portals, they were shepherded past the food refuse bins standing rudely by the central heating oil tank, and in through the kitchen. The Jap's eyes had almost hissed shut with shocked humiliation at the sight of all the cabbages and pans, but when he had to struggle past Marilyn Sidlow in the tight passage between the dishwasher and fridge he had a change of mood, and made a mental note to suggest in his report to his Chairman that the club should install a bathhouse run by girls like the one he had just rubbed against.

Now, after welcoming Sir Harold Wing also, and privately wondering what the hell he was up to, Ralphie kicked the meeting into motion. 'This is the last meeting of the Pro-Am Committee, as you know. I think we have done everything and so unless you can spot a hole in anything I say, this will just be a wrap-up and goodbye till the big day. Feel free to butt in if you see me going wrong.

'Security. This will be handled by Barrier Security of London. The Assistant Chief Constable is not over the moon about this but a compromise has been reached. His lads will do the glamour jobs, looking after celebrities, guarding the clubhouse, etc., and Barrier's lads will do the round-the-clock dirty work.

'TV, press and radio. The *Newtown Examiner* is devoting its centre-spread to the day of the event with several lead-up pieces and interviews. Radio Ranting will have a car here all day for live interviews and every member of the committee has, I believe, spoken on RR about the event.' He looked around and they nodded back. 'TV coverage is going to be difficult. The BBC say they are covering Sheepdog Trials. However, the Independent companies are still thinking about it and will let us know. They all say that Saturday is a bad day. Every national newspaper has responded to our press release with requests for more information, and I think we will have a very strong turnout.

'Catering. Dagwood Catering have provided a magnificent menu which I hope everyone will find breathtaking. It includes a buffet lunch, a seven-course Grand Dinner with lashings of fine wine and oceans of Krug '47. Champagne will in fact be served throughout the troughing, and we figure on feeding 200 and having a large glacé swan on the top table.' Turning to the yellow alien, Ralphie said, 'And I hope you will be there to join us, Mr Kinichiwa, and of course your Chairman.'

'Thank you,' replied Kinichiwa. 'We will be delighted to attend but you should know that Mr Kobiyashi, the father of our company, eats only sea urchins. He would consider that such a menu smacks of ostentation.'

The chilled silence which followed these words was made for the slimy diplomacy of Sir Harold Wing.

'Of course, of course,' he cried. 'And so do we, old chap, but remember with whom we are dealing. Sportsmen and showbiz folk, sir. Immature people who live in a schoolchild's world of make-believe.' He expressed resignation with eyebrows and shoulders. 'It's regrettable, but . . .'

'Thank you, Sir Harold,' said Ralphie quickly. 'Now the next item is insurance.

'This has been fixed with SafeHaven using the Abandonment Policy which has cost us £800. The erection of grandstands, marquees for the club and sponsors, public toilets, signposting, shops and advertising hoardings is being undertaken by Babylon SG & T Ltd. The work is progressing on schedule and the cost to the club will be £4,000. There have been the usual complaints from members about the inconvenience and cases of drunkenness amongst the construction crews but no lasting harm.'

Now Ralphie was approaching the climax of his speech. 'The biggest problem all along has been attracting top golfers and celebrities. If you'd seen the list of no-hopers the PGA first sent to us early on you would have died. To cut a long story short, after sending them a very sharp letter and using all the influence that this committee possesses, including the establishment of a major prize fund thanks to the generosity of Shin Hai Zips, I can report that we now have a line-up of sportsmen and personalities that would not disgrace a Royal Command performance. I've held the full list back just for the sheer joy of looking at your little faces as I read it out. Now. The following have accepted our invitation and are coming. Not maybes or possibles but *definites*! Are you ready? Sean Connery, Michael Caine, Val Doonican, Bruce Forsyth, Omar Sharif, Henry Cooper, Tony Jacklin, Peter Oosterhuis, Sandy Lyle, Sam Torrance, Des O'Connor, Telly Savalas, Eamonn Darcy, Ignacio de Leon, Mark James, Andrew Stubbs, Ronan Rafferty and Nick Faldo. This is, of course, not mentioning Ian Botham, Frank Bruno, Jimmy Tarbuck and Rod Stewart who have promised to come if they possibly can!'

Ralphie held out the list of acceptances and let it spin into the middle of the table. The politician had the fastest snatch and the others, with the exception of Kinichiwa who had never heard of Ignacio de Leon listened to him repeating the names.

'This is quite remarkable, Ralph. How did we manage to get them?' said Wing, craftily including himself in the entrapment team.

'How did *you* manage to get them?' asked Snodin, a more simple soul, as he and Mountford in turn gaped at the line-up.

It was the first time Ralphie had scored over Wing and he relished the chance to take a lap of honour. He waved a hand vaguely. 'It was a team effort, Bob. Hard work and good connections, generous sponsors (a brief nod here to Kinichiwa) plus our surprise charity attraction which the showbiz people obviously found irresistible.'

Privately, Ralphie thought it was a stroke of sheer genius on his part to get Shin Hai Zips, admittedly with Wing's help in the corridors of power, to sponsor a fund to equip retired bookbinders with motorized bathchairs to ferry them in their twilight years between their hovels and the Saloon Bar of the Rest and Be Buggered. Ralphie had no interest, business or otherwise, in the fate of elderly bookbinders, whom he found boring in the extreme, but could any more pathetic spectacle be conceived than a convoy of ink-stained, dribbling octogenarians parading down Bishop's Ranting High Street on the anniversary of the founding of their Bookbinders' Guild in 1668? Anyway, nauseating or not, the Nips with their cradle-to-grave employment policy had gone for it in a big way and that was what really mattered.

Part of the fund had been allocated to jacking up the prize-money at the tournament to near-Wentworth proportions, and the golf pros had been unable to refuse the offer. Once the pros were in, the Celebrities had followed like sheep, as they always did when asked to a piss-up with a bit of glitz, especially when it gave them the chance to play with star golfers.

Everyone present had known for some time of the Shin Hai deal, but Ralphie had deliberately kept quiet about the extent of his triumph with the golf pros and the Celebs. This was the part of the operation which he had run with great discretion from his Portakabin office on the Dream Rantings building site. Now he could reap the benefits of his lone campaign.

While Ralphie reflected on his cleverness, Snodin was reading the list of star names like a deposit account statement. He shook his head and whistled. 'There hasn't been a turnout like this since the Royal Wedding!'

'Yes,' said Ralphie, and could not resist adding, 'and that's not counting Terry Wogan and Paul McCartney who actually rang up to say that they would move heaven and earth to get here if it was in any way possible.

'In fact,' he continued, 'far from being the disaster which some of our derisive friends at the club bar predicted, the tournament has been so well received that we now have an accommodation problem. To solve this I have been to see the manager of the New Town Hinchcliffe. It's not the Ritz but he has said he will be delighted to accommodate our guests at a special rate for the club. We estimate a bill of about £3,500, but of course it may be less. At worst we will be paying for 30 professional golfers and about the same number of stars and their camp-followers, but weighed against this is the enormous pulling-power of their names with sponsors and the public alike.'

Ralphie paused. 'Now tell them about the hospitality tents, Rhino!' Suddenly he felt a wave of tiredness. It was getting to him. He'd worked his tripes out fixing this and pushing that and it was time he engineered himself a decent holiday. However, Rhino Hughton was as firm and fresh as ever.

'All the holes have been sold,' announced the Secretary, 'and each one has a sponsor's marquee by it. Sponsors will be held responsible for their own rubbish disposal, except Shin Hai. We'll see to that. The only black spot was Adams's Pig Farm and we never thought we were going to get rid of it to a sponsor but eventually Mr Aaron Blomberg took it. He won't get many visitors in that area, which is why I suppose he took it in the first place, but nevertheless it means we are sold out on holes and that's £18,000 in the pot. The Sheerpitts Golf Club hospitality tent will offer drinks and snacks to private guests and will have the Rantings Police Band playing during the day. In the evening, when we are assaulting the food mountain, Colonel Ooks's USAAF band will aid our digestion. There is also a 'native' ensemble playing knee-flutes which should go down very well in the hamburger tent area, which is as far away from the VIPs as possible.

'As for which club members will be playing, this has been the major topic of conversation here for weeks. Not only does everyone want to play, they also want to play with someone famous, and that's coming from members who haven't had a club in their hands since I've been here!'

Scenting a whiff of controversy, Ralphie perked up suddenly and took over the reins. 'Yes, well a lot of people are going to be disappointed, and the only way I can see us avoiding being lynched is by drawing the names out of a hat. We'll do it by lot and make a bit of a show of it. We'll have Jack Burberry supervising Marilyn doing it in a swimsuit, or something, in the presence of the Secretary and myself. It'll all be above board and the full list will be made public a couple of days before the tournament.'

Ralphie nodded vigorously to endorse the wisdom of what he had just said, and motioned to Hughton. 'Will you run through the details of the draw, Rhino.'

The Secretary, looking down at his notes, spoke slowly and distinctly as if he was addressing a class of subnormals. 'The tournament will be contested by 30 fourballs made up of a single professional and three amateurs. The first quartet will tee off at 0800 and groups will leave at ten-minute intervals, the last leaving at 1300. Those who start before noon will eat on completion of their round while those with a later start will dine on arrival. The round will be marked on the best two scores out of four and amateurs will enjoy their full handicap. Margaret Vyner-Kenty will be our only lady member playing. Altogether, 120 players will be involved starting with the 30 professionals. We haven't got a final figure on Celebrities yet but we estimate about 20 which is very good. Of the remaining 70 places, 54 go to sponsors and the remaining 16 to this club. It doesn't seem very many but some of the sponsors' nominees will also be club members so I estimate about 30 locals will be out there which looks much better. Naturally, Mr Kinichiwa, if you require more places than the three allotted to each sponsor it can be arranged. Otherwise I think that's it, Mr Chairman!'

Ralphie heaved a great sigh of relief. 'Thank you, Rhino. It is now my pleasure to turn to our major sponsor, Shin Hai Zips, and their representative here this evening, Mr Kinichiwa. As you know, the company has agreed to invest £100,000 in the Bookbinders' Guild Bathchair Fund, minus the prize-money for the tournament for which we have set aside £30,000. This generous gift of sponsorship not only guarantees Sheerpitts Golf Club a fine line-up for our tournament, it gives Shin Hai Zips an opportunity to make themselves known to the UK in general and the Rantings in particular. Perhaps Mr Kinichiwa would like to say a few words on behalf of his company. Mr Kinichiwa?'

This time their Japanese guest offered much more of a bow, and they were given an unwelcome view of his grey-stubbled, oval skull before his eyes came up to hold each of theirs in turn. Ralphie sensed that he would be more at ease addressing them standing on top of a box, but when the man started to speak he wiped his mind clean for there would be bargaining to do.

'Thank you,' said Mr Kinichiwa without feeling. 'The father of our company, Mr Kobiyashi . . . Koobee . . . ashee, sends his kindest regards and looks forward with joy to the day when he first sets foot on your fine course.' The others mumbled self-consciously in reply and he went on in faintly

* BOSS

* SEA URCHIN SHANTY

accented English: 'Although 93 years of age Mr Kobiyashi plays golf every day and he is off scratch. He is captain of the Shin Hai All Nippon champions and also plays regularly for the Shin Hai Netball and Water Polo squads. Japan is a small and overcrowded island, and the opportunity to play golf is limited and expensive. Mr Kobiyashi is a very democratic person and regularly takes his turn collecting balls on the Works driving range. There is no special parking place reserved for him in the company car park. His diet of sea urchins and rainwater keeps him in excellent physical condition for a man of his years, but since his 90th birthday he has sought a little more peace and solitude. For this purpose and for the siting of our company's European base of operations, Shin Hai representatives were sent throughout the Continent to seek a suitable location with adjacent golf course which conformed to our needs. He is a businessman as well as sportsman, poet and philanthropist, and the large subsidies and attractive tax concessions offered by the British government, allied to the proximity of Sheerpitts, made the Rantings and your club our choice and Mr Kobiyashi your benefactor.

'When news of your great charity tournament came to us through Sir Harold, we suggested sponsorship to Mr Kobiyashi and he could not wait to give.'

Mr Kinichiwa paused, and was rewarded by a burst of applause all round the table. When it had subsided he returned to his brief. 'He will present the cheque for £100,000 personally to your nominee. In retrn for this sincere gift he would be most happy to be offered the captaincy of your club next year.' The avalance of gratitude became a glacier and the room temperature plummetted. 'He would also be deeply moved by the granting of membership to the following senior management of Shin Hai Zips: Mr Sato Omichigata, Mr Toru Shigetsu, Mr Hideko Tomi-Harakashi, Mr Hirri Yorukawa, Mr Soryu Shindo, Mr Sakai Fugata, Mr Hara Mitsukarita, Mr Tanaka Sunichisaki, Mr Ito Sunichisaki, and . . . (he raised a small hand to his chest) Mr Nobosuke Kinichiwa.'

Kinichiwa looked around to the table to judge the impact of his request, but it was difficult to gauge. Dammit, you could never tell with these Occidentals and their deep-set eyes and open mouths. They seemed happy enough. He tried again. 'Do you like poetry?' he asked carefully. They looked at Ralphie in strangled horror but before he could find an answer Sir Harold spoke for all. 'Yes. We love it dearly!' he said, looking meaningfully at the committee. Kinichiwa relaxed with a smile.

'Mr Kobiyashi is famous in Japan for reciting his own verse. He says it is poor but he asks me to give you each a bound copy of his single-line golf poem 'Thoughts on replacing a divot'. From his breast pocket he removed six pencil-thin rolls of paper wrapped in fine red silk ribbon which he passed carefully around. 'Please read in the privacy of your own home.

Mr Kobiyashi is a strong believer in the depth and strength of thinking necessary for complete appreciation of the game of golf and it is compulsory for all management levels at Shin Hai. He also feels that there should be on every golf course a quiet place where a player can sit and examine his oneness with the game. Mr Kobiyashi often stands in driving winter rain clad only in a short Budoka for hours thinking of the patterns in bunker sand after it has been smoothed by the careful, considerate golfer. "It is Enough" is our company motto and this is worth thinking on. We have examined a map of the Sheerpitts course and suggest that the discreet siting of an unobtrusive shrine near the 5th or 6th hole could not possibly offend Christian members.'

Ralphie squirmed in his seat trying to catch the MP's eyes but he was writing something. 'Er, no . . . Mr Kinichiwa,' he managed to reply, 'we'd have to set up, er, a Shrine Committee, but I can't see any, er . . .'

Wing was surreptitiously holding up his notebook. The message read, 'Give him the Moon.'

Kinichiwa was now showing signs of genuine emotion and without instruction from above he blurted out, 'The water hazard at the 14th. Sheerpitts Lake. It is possible that you would give permission to replace the rough railway sleepers with a delicate ornamental bridge in the style of the Meiji emperors? Mr Kobiyashi is an expert on the period and would be delighted.'

Ralphie waved his arms in a bra removing motion. 'No trouble . . . Nobbie. Anything you want!'

Kinichiwa now laughed out aloud. 'The serving maid in the kitchen. When the presence of Shin Hai in the area is accepted . . . all Japanese golf clubs have bathhouses.'

'Everything is possible,' the Chairman said, and then with a flash of recognition as he noticed Sir Harold's hand perform a fly-squashing manoeuvre, 'but I don't think we should rush things too much, eh!'

The arrow struck home in a vital spot and Kinichiwa was correctly mortified. 'Of course. Thank you. This has been a most enlightening meeting. It is permitted for me to leave before its conclusion? Mr Kobiyashi expects a report from me.'

Wing accepted the offer and they all rose. 'Of course, old chap, and thank you for coming. The gift from Mr Kobiyashi is most welcome and please convey our sincere thanks. We look forward to seeing him here in the clubhouse and on the course. Now we have some private business to discuss. Captain Hughton, would you . . . ?'

Hughton moved to the door, opened it and checked for the Brigadier. Turning, he shook his head and gestured for the Deputy Managing-Director of Shin Hai Zips to follow him. Kinichiwa shook hands with the shell-shocked Tournament Committee and left the room. When he had gone they looked at each other, shaking their heads. Snodin was the first to say it.

'Who the hell do they think they are? Ornamental bridges! Shrines! What was the lunatic talking about? This is a golf club, not a Willow-pattern plate. I've never heard anything as mad as that in my life. Is the man ill?'

He looked around for an answer and Mountford gave it, shaking his head furiously. 'They can't have the faintest notion about golf. He never mentioned the bar once.'

'Not surprised, old man,' Snodin said through his handkerchief. 'They're only small people. Basic metabolism isn't up to it. One drink and the little buggers are legless. Mark my words, once they get in here we'll be drinking green tea at the bar, and that will really please the Brigadier. I can't say that I've ever liked the man, but when you think about all the things he's said about Japs, he's absolutely right!'

Ralphie said nothing, and when he glanced over at Wing the leonine head urgently indicted a return to the table. Hughton came back to join them, and before the complaints reached a level of pure hysteria the MP sought to reassure them.

'Gentlemen, he began, I have no standing on this committee and really shouldn't be saying anything but if I could have your attention for a few minutes, perhaps I can indicate a path forward. In my duties as your MP I regularly come into contact with foreign trade missions as part of the never-ending battle to attract work to the Rantings, and the Japs are no different to the rest, believe me. If it's the Americans they want ice cold drinks and bloody hamburgers, if it's the Hun you're being mown down by fleets of blasted Mercedes . . .' The warm understanding voice smoothed their tensions into wrinkles of relaxation and laughter and for the hundredth time Ralphie thought, 'I've got to watch this bugger or he'll have me.' '. . . but at the end of the day it's *our* country and there are more of us here than there are of them so I don't think we should get too upset about their somewhat eccentric requests!'

Snodin's doubt still blistered his good humour and he leaned forward. 'But, Sir Harold, he didn't seem to be joking when he spoke of a shrine out there! People don't joke about religion, especially Eastern fanatics. How long will it be before we have monks chanting and setting fire to themselves on a lovely summer's day because they've four-putted the 5th?'

It seemed a perfectly logical question and Ralphie put his chin in his hands to hear the answer. Wing was hugely reassuring.

'I don't think it will ever get to that stage, Bob. I can't see the Brigadier allowing a Japanese shrine to last long at Sheerpitts, can you? Or even a Colonel Ooks Wayside Yodelling Pulpit for that matter!'

They were his again and Ralphie had to smile.

'What the Japs want is no problem,' continued the MP. 'I suggest we pocket the money and say yes to everything they desire until they go over the top and ask for too much, which everybody does eventually. Ralph will then feed the story to the local press, the nationals will be onto it like rats up a drainpipe and the next day it'll be: "JAPS THREATEN PRECIOUS GOLFING HERITAGE. TEE HOUSE CEREMONY DEMAND". Then they'll have to back down or lose face, so you have no worries on that score, believe me.'

They did, and minutes later six much happier men headed for the bar.

Blomberg's Progress

The double doors leading from the club bar to the terrace were jammed with bodies. Clutching their pre-lunch drinks at collarbone height and chattering excitedly they scanned the path from the locker room to the 1st tee.

'Here he comes!' a voice yelled and with a strangled cheer the portal-bound crush burst free followed by the drinkers packed behind them. The well dressed mob surged out into the open piling up in waves behind the low wall which overlooked the start of all of Aaron Blomberg's most public humiliations. The cheering turned to hysterical laughter as his next opponent in the Vase Competition appeared and gravely acknowledged the welcome with a fruity blast on his bulb motor horn.

Sam Cuddy was wearing his six-year-old son's green plastic crash helmet, a red-and-yellow hooped Rantings Mental Home Rugby jersey and black tights. Cuddy was a partner in a firm of New Town undertakers and ran Archie Gosling close in the race to alcoholic oblivion. His golf, however, was not up to the same standard, and after playing several times in rolled-up shirt-sleeves he had been called before the Standards and General Practices Committee to be cautioned

about his casual attitude to dress on the course. He had also been told that Sheerpitts was a golf club not a circus, and if he erred once more he would be severely dealt with. Blomberg, who had watched the carnival in amazement, looked down at his own impeccable canary cashmere sweater and well filled tartan trousers through bitter tears. Over the wall the entire SG&P committee tried to support each other in helpless mirth as Cuddy approached Aaron, bowed three times, knelt in silent prayer and, after shaking hands, accepted the honour.

Blomberg looked around wildly for justice as Sam placed an ancient ball on a six-inch peg and addressed it with a child's pink plastic putter, his rear end jutting out at a ridiculous angle and balancing on one leg. 'Mr Secretary, Colonel Beam, this is not fair! Surely such conduct . . .'

Hughton drew back into the crowd and Beam was at the bar replenishing a gin and tonic spilled from his hand in the stampede to see and humiliate the innocent. Dear Old Jack Burberry said something but it was drowned by happy comment from the audience. 'Where's your sense of humour, Bumberg? You shouldn't have joined if you can't take a joke. Get on with it!' Further advice was lost in the delirium as Cuddy slipped a condom over his driver, assumed the skier's egg position and sliced the ball in a whirring arc in the direction of the greenkeeper's hut. Sam fell to the ground dead, rose to do a funny walk and finally gestured for Aaron to repeat the exercise.

Blomberg was deeply offended but he knew that it was the old story, and he could only follow Norman Cooper's strict instructions to play the course and not his opponent or, in this instance, the entire club. He turned inward and began to recite the 'Prayers for the Dead' as he pegged his Cooper 666 and addressed it. The delighted watchers, hearing the quiet chant, joined cheerfully in with him but he ignored them as his atrocious backswing inched towards its apogee. The clubhead froze long enough for a passing inquiry from a fly before it began its viciously kinked downswing. A shout of delight greeted its return to a position level with his left hip and eager fingers indicated to him the ball's resting place: ten feet from the tee.

Aaron opened his eyes and felt the sweat flood into them. He couldn't go on like this. Not for his father or Uncle Sol, not for his tailoring business, not even for the row of orange trees named after him in Tel Aviv.

'Want me to play again?' Sam inquired pleasantly, taking off his plastic crash helmet.

'You're breaking the rules, Mr Cuddy, and I'm going to claim this match!' Blomberg's remark was overheard and the crowd quietened. He summoned up his courage and said, 'I would like Mr Cooper to come here, please, or anyone who knows the rules of the game. It's my right!'

McNish leaned over the wall. 'I know this game, laddie,' he said, 'and while I don't go much for fooling about in silly clothing I don't think you have anything to complain about. I suggest you get on with it or Mr Cuddy will be the winner.'

Awakened from an early session with the Glenmorangie and attracted by the noise, Norman Cooper excused himself through the crowd. 'What is it, gentlemen? It's too nice a day for arguments. Can I be of any assistance?'

Relieved that a friend had arrived, Blomberg wiped his brow as the professional looked genially at Cuddy. Norman knew exactly what it was all about. They were trying to humiliate and stuff his pupil and there was absolutely nothing he could do about it. Sam could dress exactly as he liked on the course if he was playing someone universally disliked by the rest of the membership and poor old Blomberg would just have to swallow the insult.

'He's claiming the match because of my style of dress, Cooper,' Cuddy laughed. 'But everyone who knows and loves me is aware that I have a delightfully quirky sense of humour and if he's so bloody sensitive . . .'

'You tell him, Sammy!' someone shouted, and the clown went for Aaron's jugular.

'He's got no place in the company of men,' went on Cuddy, 'and should sod off back to Tel Aviv!' This was a bit strong but still ignited warm applause. 'I am playing as I am, and if he doesn't like it all he has to do is give me the match and buy me a large drink!'

He looked at Blomberg and then at Cooper with a smile. Cooper turned to Aaron. 'Mr Blomberg . . .' What the hell was he going to say to a man who was averaging thirty lessons a week and needed more. The problem was that if he got really peeved, as he had every right to do at the unfair and discriminatory treatment being handed out to him in public, he might leave the club and bang goes the pension.

'Mr Cooper,' the professional's pension asked quietly, 'how Mr Cuddy wishes to dress, even though I am a bespoke tailor and it hurts, is of no concern to me. I claim the match on other grounds. How many clubs is a player permitted to carry in his bag. Fourteen, I think?' Aaron pointed a thick forefinger at his opponent's bag. 'Mr Cuddy is carrying fifteen!'

The crowd, alarmed, inched forward to listen and Cuddy reacted angrily as Archie Gosling fell over the wall unnoticed. 'What's he on about?' he said brutally and Cooper's heart leapt with hope.

'Surely you haven't got an extra club in your bag, Mr Cuddy? One, two, three . . . seven, eight, nine . . . oh dear, that looks like fifteen to me. Including this.'

Cooper pointed to the pink plastic putter. Sam stared at him, then bellowed with laughter and waved the pink implement in the air. 'You don't mean this, do you? It's a toy. It belongs to my little boy, Frankie!'

Cooper bent over as the crowd roared and cheered derisively, and when he straightened he was holding Cuddy's tee peg in his hand. The owner's humour dried on his lips. 'I know what you're going to say. Yes, I used that but it was only a joke!'

Cuddy's face was reddening and Cooper could see a chance of at least awarding the hole to Blomberg and getting him away from the clubhouse ghouls. 'Mr Blomberg's right, Mr Cuddy. This is a club and it is the fifteenth in your bag, so . . .'

'So I am claiming the match. Blomberg is the winner!' Aaron said in the style of Napoleon after the Battle of Austerlitz.

Cooper raised his hands. 'Don't spoil it, you turkey!' he mouthed at his mature student. 'No, Mr Blomberg,' he went on out loud, 'for carrying an extra club your opponent will be penalized one hole, not the entire match.'

Cuddy marched forward and shook his finger under Blomberg's nose. 'You can have the hole. He can have the hole. HE CAN HAVE THE BLOODY HOLE. I WAS CARRYING AN EXTRA CLUB WHICH I NOW SHOW YOU ALL BEFORE SLINGING IT INTO THE CAR PARK. YOUR HOLE, MR BLOODY BLOMBERG, AND NOW I AM GOING TO SKIN THE ARSE OFF YOU. PROCEED!'

Before he could fling the plastic club amongst the Sierras, Aaron touched his arm. 'I am claiming the match, Mr Cuddy. That putter, which you have just admitted to all and sundry was one of your clubs, has, I believe, a concave putting surface which is illegal! Mr Cooper?'

Cooper was in a daze as he looked at the pink object. 'He's right, you know,' he said. 'It's a concave little bugger!'

Cuddy went crimson. 'That's RIDICULOUS!' he said through welling tears, but Norman relentlessly adhered to the Rules of Golf.

'It is an illegal club, Mr Cuddy, and I'm afraid you forfeit the match. It is concave, as you cannot deny.'

Cooper held the club briefly aloft before Cuddy snatched it from him and flung it towards the car park. 'Wait till I get home!' he screamed, 'I'll kill the little sod!'

He lurched off leaving his trolley abandoned. The crowd was silent and uncertain what to do. Sam suddenly stopped and whirled on them. 'What are you lot gaping at? Piss off!' he instructed them fiercely, and they did, leaving Blomberg safely in the semi-finals – and a hundred more lessons to be entered in Norman Cooper's little book.

COUNTDOWN

Ralphie Jukes confides his true feelings to an old chum.

'**T**his is Radio Rantings' Peter Pallet, and I'm at Sheerpitts Golf Club talking to the man who has almost singlehandedly put together what promises to be the biggest event to happen in the Rantings since Algernon Poyning's Great Pie Massacre! Yes, it's the Shin Hai Pro-Am Charity Golf Classic, and I'm talking to well-known local builder and businessman Mr Ralph Jukes who is wearing yet another hat today, that of Tournament Director! This ferociously busy gentleman has taken a few minutes off from final preparations for the big wing-ding, which is due to start in less than 48 hours time, to talk to us and choose seven of his all-time favourite musical hits. Radio Ranting will be covering the golf for you and speaking to the host of stars and sportsmen who will shortly be treading this historical greensward in aid of the ageing members of our famous Guild. Mr Jukes, how are things going as the great day approaches?'

'Call me Ralphie, Peter. Well, I must say that everything is rolling along nicely! It has been a tremendous job of organization for such a small club as ours but we've had 100 per cent backing from the members and I'm blessed with a really hard-working and determined Committee.'

'I noticed what a lot of local bookbinders are calling the "Field of the Cloth of Gold", Ralphie. A great tented village. That must have taken some planning?'

'Well, I've never heard of that before but, yes, the erection of sponsors' tents and large marquees where, we hope, most of the good folk of The Rantings will come to enjoy a pint of Monks and pies and hamburgers, has taken some laying out. We're particularly proud of the – did you see it when you came in? – the big 500-seater temporary grandstand on the last green?'

'Very impressive, Ralphie. The place has been a hive of activity lately and it would do some of those people, who are always knocking the British workman, good to see how your chaps have got into the job. Has there been much interruption to the normal running of the club?'

'A little, but the members have been most understanding. There's bound to be some inconvenience but as soon as they realized that it was for the good of the Rantings they happily accepted it.'

'Typical of our great community spirit, of course. Well, Ralphie, the whole place looks magnificent, and it will look even better when it's lit up with the galaxy of talent that you and your committee have enticed to the fair Rantings. Sean Connery, Bruce Forsyth, Michael Caine and many others.'

'Yes, the support has been magnificent. Everyone who promised to come

is coming and we have some mystery celebrities who are hoping to make it plus a last-minute attraction, the Victor Sylvester Memorial Free-Fall Formation Dance Team. The way things are going I wouldn't be in the least surprised if there wasn't a hint of Royalty in the air . . .'

'Ralphie, let's have that again! Ladies and gentlemen, this could be a World Scoop for Radio Rantings. Are you saying that there is a possibility of a member of the Royal Family visiting this part of the Rantings in the near future . . . oh fuck! This bloody machine is absolutely useless! It hasn't recorded a word we've said!'

'Pete, I told you didn't I? I said I could pick up good-quality cheap Japanese stuff which will never let you down! I can get you . . .'

'Ralphie, you got me this bastard, remember?'

'Oh, well, don't worry, I'll replace it. There's some good stuff coming in from the States shortly . . . bloody hell, that almost slipped my mind! This golf thing is driving me up the wall!'

'How is it going?'

'It's a bloody shambles. Marilyn . . . MARILYN! Two Scotches! Quick! You don't know what it's been like!'

'Have the members been giving you a hard time? They're a miserable bunch of sods. There was talk of drunkenness among the scaffolding crowd.'

'Yes. I don't know where they got it. Couple of broken legs amongst 'em too, which cheered the membership up somewhat. Apparently, Tina Gurning came by to have a nose round, and two of the silly buggers fell off the top of the big stand when she breathed in!'

'I'd have fallen with them. How can she be married to that poor sod. Is he still sleeping in the greenkeeper's hut?'

'Yes. You know what the biggest problem was?'

'Lifting injured scaffolders off Tina Gurning?'

'Poor old Blomberg. They've cheated him out of playing in the Charity Vase Final. You know, the feller I managed to slip in under the wire.'

'Yes, the tailor. What d'you mean? There was some talk in the pub about him going through the competition like . . .'

'He's the worst golfer who ever mishit a ball, but by a collection of miracles he somehow managed to reach the final of the competition. He even overcame the She-monster!'

'They said that but I didn't believe it. What a cow!'

'My friend Aaron struck a blow for all men everywhere, but the General Purposes Committee didn't like the idea of someone like him appearing in the final just before such a prestigious affair as the Pro-Am, so it was decided that because of the pressure on the course, groundstaff, etc., the competition would be held over to a later date.'

'I thought the winner was entitled to a place in the Pro-Am?'

'True, but they asked Archie Gosling, the other finalist, believe it or not, and he said he didn't mind missing out if it was for the good of the club, etc, etc. Actually, he had no idea what they were talking about at the time.'

'And Blomberg. What did the poor sod say? He's down as a sponsor, isn't he?'

'He was furious, but as he was entitled to play as a sponsor there wasn't a lot he could do about it. They just didn't want him to play in the final, and if he withdrew his sponsorship at such a late stage it would be a great excuse to drum him out of the club, so he just had to swallow it.'

GOLF BALL LOSES TEMPER WITH MAN

A Great Ranting woman dressed as a giant golf ball lost her temper and repeatedly punched a man after he asked whether it was her or the golf ball who was 65, Bishop's Ranting magistrates were told today.

Amanda Pringle, 25, unemployed of Hinchcliffe Gardens, Bishop's Ranting New Town, admitted assaulting Geoffrey Greenfield, causing actual bodily harm. Mr Russell Bone, prosecuting, said the pair were part of a group gathered in New Town Plaza shopping precinct, when Pringle started to play around by bumping the man with her costume.

Mr Greenfield later told police that he had offered the woman some lemonade, which she refused saying he might have AIDS. The accused admitted that he threw lemonade over her and called her brother names.

Asked from the bench why the accused was dressed in such a manner, Ms Victoria Price for the accused said Pringle was a member of the 'FREE CHARLIE PRINGLE CAMPAIGN' and had planned to draw attention to her brother's alleged wrongful imprisonment on a trumped-up charge, by halting traffic in the High Street.

Pringle was given a conditional discharge, fined £200 and ordered to pay £75 costs. Police were called to collect 422 golf balls found in the court, and they were placed in the custody of the chairman of the bench, Brigadier Patterson, VC, JP.

'Are you expecting any trouble from the Pringles? Looks like the perfect occasion for one of their super-demos. You know they've sworn to place rolls of specially treated toilet paper in the New Town supermarkets if Charlie's case isn't reviewed soon? He *was* innocent wasn't he?'

'Yes. Dowty fitted him up for the job here but he's done hundreds of others. I don't know what they're getting so upset about! When Charlie was home, the police were always there breaking up fights.'

'Ralphie, let's talk about a couple of other things. What's the weather report for your big do? I don't want to be interviewing Henry Cooper in the pissing rain.'

'The long-range weather says that it's going to be fine. Clear and sunny with light winds. Couldn't be better!'

'Which means I'll be interviewing our Enery in the pissing rain. So what do you think about that?'

'That would be perfect.'

'What! Are you serious.'

'Of course, I'm serious. The last thing I want is this place jammed solid with superstars and the likes of you eating and drinking like it's become compulsory. I don't want the reeking masses of Bishop's Ranting New Town here either. My idea of heaven would be for God to speak to me and say, 'Ralphie, go forth and build an ark because I am going to drop 56 inches of rain on your head. I will give you this warning so that you will have enough time to telephone all of the world's free-loaders and tell them to stay at home and eat and drink their own produce for a change, and also to enable you to take a well earned rest. Amen.'

'I thought that was the way you felt. I've seen what happens at charity dos. Well, let's hope that there's a nice little cloudburst at about teatime the day before, and the place is under water. Do you want to give the chat another go? I think I saw a flicker of life in this pile of junk! Yes, it's working. I'll ask you about the weather report, Celebs and how much it'll cost to get in. Oh, can you fix me and Val up with tickets for the Celebrity Dinner at the club? Val's brother-in-law and his wife would also like to come if you can swing it, and do you think there's any chance that our Ronnie could carry Jimmy Tarbuck's bag? Personally I can't stand the bloke but our Ronnie . . . Oh, it's the totally delicious Marilyn! Thanks, luv.'

Blomberg's Progress

Sixty-four members had put their names down to play in the Vase Knockout Competition, a record for any club event, and now the number had been whittled down, by slices, hooks, shanks, hangovers, illegalities and death, to four. The semi-final draw had been made by Jack Burberry, held up by his faithful President-elect, Ralphie Jukes, and the pairings were ideal. Reaching for the four slips of tightly screwed-up paper deep in the black velvet bag which was, Ken Dowty alleged, the same one slipped over the brewery chief's head by his girlfriend in moments of intimacy, Jack had coupled Jock McGee and

Archie Gosling with his first feeble gropings. Margaret Vyner-Kenty's heart had bounced about her chest for it meant that she was to play Blomberg and thus be guaranteed a place in the final, and a front seat at Armageddon.

At last, after years of transcendental meditation, pumping iron and selflessly denying herself any of life's pleasures, a kindly fortune had smiled on her. She had been given the chance to strike a memorable blow for women by defeating the drunken lout who epitomized all that the male members of Sheerpitts Golf Club found so worthy and admirable. It was undeniable that he was an

opponent supreme, an effortless striker of a golf
ball who read fairways and greens with the same
casual regard as the garish labels on the bottles
clinking in his bag, but yes! she knew that she
could beat him! The man was always so drunk
that he could hardly totter to the tee, and often
had to be helped. There was no way that such a
drunken sot was going to beat her and she aimed
to win by any means in the rule book.

She studied the dos and don'ts night after night
and could find nothing prohibiting him from
drinking. She couldn't even nail him on
unsporting conduct because he did nothing to
unsettle his partner. He did in fact do everything,
on the face of it, to give his opponent more of a fair
chance than the rules demanded, so she had no
hope on the alcohol front. He was a slow player
but invariably had to wait for his opponent's
second and third shots to catch up with his first,
which again permitted her no complaint. He was
punctual, dressed civilly and did not cheat. His
card marking was sometimes a little mazy and
hard to read, but he was hardly alone in that.
There was no doubt about it, to win she had to
play the round better than he did, and even
though he was off scratch and giving her two
strokes per hole, she didn't think she could do it.

No, his defeat could only be brought about by
personal misdemeanours and the sole weakness
she could play on was also his greatest strength:
alcohol. She had wracked her brains since the
draw trying to evolve a plan that would either
encourage him to drink too much or not enough.
From what she had seen of him at the bar, and on
the course, Too Much only fired him to greater
feats so it had to be Not Enough. Somehow she
had to deny him his drinks at the bar prior to their
setting out, or pray that they started playing
before the bar opened. Hughton worked out the
starting times, and she knew he hated her guts so
all she could do was hope.

Her second-phase plan was more tangible and
promising. It required the engineering of an
accident involving someone like the large Mrs
Protheroe and her trolley colliding with Archie
and his vehicle, the outcome being fatal damage to
the liquid cargo on the male golfer's trolley. Sadly,
the lady of the 5 o'clock shadow (which was a
genuine room darkener) might prove
uncooperative, for since that disgusting boy had
been taking her into the woods her attitude to Mr
Protheroe and men in general had mellowed.

Margaret's friend Dorothy would be a better bet.
If only she had a little more poke, *that* much more
dedication, she would prove to be a worthy
partner in the war of the sexes; this could be her
watershed. One way or the other, a bruising
encounter would be arranged which, if all went
well, would leave Archie without travelling
comfort. On the move he would become helpless
but the next problem would be the caches of
bottles at every hole.

The Lady Captain was toying with a plan, a
very risky plan, of conceding the first four holes
before they reached the green where she knew the
treasures waited. She assessed that after twenty
minutes without alcohol his game would be in
rags and that she would be able to make up the
deficit comfortably. If he really fell to pieces she
might conceivably give away the first *eight* and
come home like a tiger! It all looked extremely
viable and she knew that with careful planning
and the tiniest spot of luck she could pull it off!

All that stood between her and everlasting
glory at that moment was the pathetic fat man
rooting around in Wayne's Wood for his 11th lost
ball of the round. Normally she would have
subjected Blomberg to one of her looks every time
their eyes met, but the leisurely pace of the game
gave her time to scrutinize her future plans for any
obvious flaws. At this hole, however, the
wretched Blomberg was spending an age swishing
disconsolately about in the damp grass, and she
had an hour on the Heavy Bullworker booked for
3 o'clock at the New Town Adonis Centre. 'Put
another one down, Mr Blomberg, or we'll be here
till dark!' she called, not for the first time.

His game was atrocious, as was the weird
chanting every time he faced a ball, and she
wondered contemptuously how much that other
whisky soak, Cooper, was screwing out of the
poor fool. At the bar they were saying that
Blomberg was coming up to his Cinquecentenary
of lessons and that the club should demonstrate
some recognition of the milestone. Blomberg
burned in effigy had been the most popular
suggestion so far, which just about typified their
Third Form thinking. 'Come on, Mr Blomberg,
please, or will you concede the hole?'

Aaron stiffened and shouted, 'No!' He moved
to the fringe of the fairway and dropped a ball
which ran gratefully into the cruel scar of an
ankle-deep divot. He looked down at the white
scalp of his target and, chanting quietly, addressed

it with all of his might. His 8-iron retired jerkily to a point below his right elbow and waited. He wobbled and then scythed the club forward. The ball rose in a screaming arc, and the astonished Margaret watched it home in on the waiting green. The white spot fell precisely in line with the flag, bounced, and with much obliging backspin came to a halt two inches from the cup.

'Did you see that?' Blomberg cried to the world as he ran for the green, his trolley bucking like a gun carriage. 'Mr Cooper was right. What a shot!'

It had been a superlative approach from an impossible lie and, as the elated idiot charged by, Miss Vyner-Kenty was forced to acknowledge this with a curt nod. Pity really, because there was no chance of him winning the hole. The masterstroke had been his ninth shot, or was it his tenth, and she was about to play her third. It was a straightforward approach and she could go for the flag or settle for being near the green. Blomberg was standing directly in her line and she shouted angrily. He turned, smiling, gave her an unseeing wave and walked to the back of the green, never taking his eyes off his ball. There was no point in talking to the man, thought Margaret. She selected a 9-iron and strolled over to her ball which was sitting comfortably in the centre of the fairway. Looking down at it, she went through the pre-shot checklist. Feet, hands, head. All correct. When the right moment came and she was composed, her hips began to uncoil and the clubhead . . . With a mind-blanking, terrifying shriek, two F15A jets flashed past only feet over her head. The sun blinked for a nanosecond and they were gone, wheeling away over the trees. The maddening, hammering blankets of sound blundered after them and Margaret was left paralyzed, her mouth open and her Snelgrove-white teeth drying in a light breeze. Slowly the scrambled senses began to draw fearfully together and she heard screaming.

It was herself. No, there was someone else. It was her *and* another woman. Margaret Vyner-Kenty stopped her own screaming and turned her head in an effort to locate the awful racket. She saw Mrs Ferris, wearing only one stocking, running wildly towards her from the wood. She was clearly demented with aero-shock, and waved her arms in the air to ward off any following attack. In the time that it took Margaret to close her mouth, Mrs Ferris hit her like a train and they both went down in a blue-film clinch.

Mrs Ferris rose immediately, untroubled by the fall, and dashed off still howling back into the wood where Wayne, hopping in one leg of his jeans, brought her down with a gentle rugby tackle and soothed away her horror.

Aaron still stared at the ball and its unbelievable proximity to the hole. He had just hit the best shot of his golfing life and hadn't noticed the sky ripping apart. From a divot as deep as the Grand Canyon he had dropped the pill *here!* The thing had stayed up there longer than a kestrel, and it was the only stroke he had ever played which he had followed from just after contact to full stop. For this unlikely event his wife had insisted he carry a camera, and rummaging in the bag pocket he found it. He would ask the woman he was playing with to snap him going for the putt. She was a miserable, bloodless creature but surely she wouldn't deny his request. 'Miss Vyner-Kenty!' he shouted as he turned. 'Could I ask you for a favour . . .'

Margaret was lying prone where he had last seen her, still clutching her club but completely motionless. He trotted over to the body. 'Miss Vyner-Kenty? Margaret . . .' There was no response and he bent down to look at her more carefully. In repose she looked no better, and he compared her to his own ample partner. She must have fainted. They were always doing it in his home when they couldn't have their own way, and probably that last shot of his had really set her hopes back with a jolt. She was breathing quickly and he touched her right shoulder compassionately. She cried out in pain and opened her eyes. 'Are you alright?' he asked as she tried to sit up, but then fell back with a groan of agony.

'Stay still,' Aaron advised, but again she struggled up and this time reached a shaky kneeling position, gingerly holding her shoulder and sucking in litres of air.

'My shoulder! What happened? Those aircraft! Oh God, did they crash?'

Blomberg looked around. 'What aircraft?'

There was no blazing wreckage on the 7th, 8th, 9th or 6th, and round the other way none on or near the 4th, 2nd or 3rd. The sky, also, was empty.

'Aircraft went over. Right above my . . . Oooh, my shoulder. Dammit this hurts. Did I see a nude . . .?'

'Pardon?' Aaron said politely.

'Nothing. Aaaah! Give me a hand!'

He took her left hand hesitantly. 'Are you sure you should try to get up? You look very . . .'

Margaret gritted her teeth as the pain from her right shoulder froze the arm then spiked into her brain. 'For God's sake, man, do as I ask. I'm going to finish this round. Pull, dammit!' She staggered upright and swayed. 'Now give me that 9-iron,' she said through white lips.

Still holding her, Aaron reached down, picked up the club and pressed it into her sweating palm.

'Where's my ball?' she asked faintly.

'In front of you,' replied Aaron, and she located it down there on ground which was swimming between her feet.

'Let go of me, dammit,' ordered the Lady Captain. 'I don't want to hit you!'

Aaron moved off a yard. 'I was going to ask you if you'd take a photograph of me holing out . . . Margaret?'

Through the electric rods of pain spreading throughout her body every time she moved, she saw Aaron's round beaming face. Why was he carrying a golf bag full of bricks up and down the stairs of her spartan home? Now he was Archie

Gosling, falling over and standing up. Oh my God, had there been aircraft? 'Get out of the way, you idiot!' she shouted at Aaron, but now the face was that of Wayne Summers. The fat little tailor had metamorphosed into the utterly beautiful boy. Oh God, he'd come for her! She was the latest virgin to be sacrificed on his bloodstained altar of lust.

'Are you feeling alright, Miss Vyner-Kenty?' Wayne asked (for it *was* he). Mrs Ferris was now much better and walking back to the clubhouse, and Wayne had thought there might be something he could do for the Lady Captain.

'You bastard!' Margaret cried, and swung the club at his golden head. He caught her before she hit him, and she passed out. After a brief pause for hole-side photography, Wayne and Aaron carried her back to the clubhouse where Dr McNish relocated her shoulder with some relish before allowing her home in the company of her friend Dorothy Bathouse. Aaron reported the result of his semi-final and also went home.

At the club they were very understanding about the incident, and the following match result was posted on the noticeboard:

VASE COMPETITION *Semi-final*
Blomberg bt Vyner-Kenty (Miss) Unable to complete the round owing to injury. Everyone at the club wishes her a swift and complete recovery.

THE GREAT DAY

Sheerpitts Golf Club goes for the big one, and some would argue that they made it.

The professional golfers and their wives and families poured into The Rantings. They were closely followed by the Celebrities and their dear ones and some close friends. Last of the Great came the Superstars closely attended by wives, families, girlfriends, boyfriends, agents, PR men, hairdressers, masseuses, financial advisers, close friends, remote friends and people they were hoping to impress.

Thicker than iron filings on a magnet came the press, represented by ghost writers, photographers, gossip writers and sports commentators. When the great wave hit the beach and receded, a smaller ripple of non-Celebrities slipped in. They were politicians, showbiz doctors and lawyers, cartoonists, writers, breakfast radio and television presenters and failed nonentities of every religious and artistic persuasion. They were place-seekers,

'… IT'S THE WEATHERMAN. YOU KNOW… "'CLEAR SKIES WITH TEMPERATURES IN THE UPPER 80's…'

apple-polishers and ego-rubbers. They were camp-followers and tent-robbers. They had scripts to sell, ideas freshly stolen, manuscripts to be read and cravings which only the great and famous could cure with a prescription signed by a flourishing autograph.

The Ranting Orbital had never been so busy and Bishop's Ranting railway station had to take on an extra tea lady. The *Ranting Examiner* sold out its first edition and Radio Ranting transmitted more traffic news than pop music for the first time in its history. Crowds of mute Rantonians stood like rows of supermarket grapefruit, their pale faces forming astonished 'O's as they lined up three deep outside the New Town Hinchcliffe to gape at the smooth easygoing familiar faces which ignored them with crushing contempt as they entered through the green glass doors to pick up the keys to their free rooms.

To begin with there was some confusion in the hotel, and soon this changed to chaos. The allotted rooms agreed with Sheerpitts Golf Club were obviously too few and the hotel manager, besotted with the quality and notoriety of his guests, welcomed them brazenly, seeking only a signature bequeathing all debts to the Tournament Account. The crowd in the lobby grew bigger and while some stars took the delay with the understanding their public expected of them and slipped over the bar to meet old friends, others grew testy and threatened to leave and not forget how they had been treated. All were eventually processed and when it came to the second, third and fourth assault waves the wretched hotel staff took them in without question as long as the bill could be safely directed at Sheerpitts Golf Club. The lifts rose and fell, rich in real leather luggage, clanking golf bags and Celebrities eager for a quick splash and then down to the bar.

Within an hour the noise from Hinchcliffe's Hideaway was stupendous and the heat and cigar smoke could be detected from Old Rantings Police Station three streets away. Dry ginger and tonic water ran out after another hour had passed and fresh supplies were hurried over from the Rest and Be Buggered. At nearly midnight the happy, shouting, joke-telling, sweating multitude demanded dinner. When the manager regretted that he could only supply sandwiches at this moment in time, the hungry, like a giant fist, punched their way through the hardiest of the gaping simpletons still waiting outside and, moved by primeval instinct, surged blindly towards the Beijing Lotus Flower Restaurant in Lower Junkin Street. It was overwhelmed in a trice and the staff, reinforced with retired waiters called from their drugged sleep, threw themselves into paper-wrapping prawns and precious-egging perfectly ordinary omelettes to meet the insatiable and noisy demand. Even the sharp cries of the waiters were lost in the furious babble when, denied the pleasure of a Chinese meal because of the Beijing's miserly 550-seat capacity, the chairless surged onward to the nearby Srikkanth Shastri and its Latin counterpart Zia Concettina da Roma.

Police officers despatched to survey the scene and collect autographs for their wives later agreed after visiting all three establishments that even when drunk the English made more noise when eating in a Chinese restaurant than they do in Indian, Italian, French, Hungarian or any other type of eating house. Two hours later the first to feel the pace rose and left to return to the hotel, followed at intervals by the more determined and those able to pay. They arrived at the Hinchcliffe at short intervals causing the night porter to open the front door 178 times, and to hand out more Alka Seltzer tablets and condoms than ever before. Many did not come back at all. Three lay in the arms of the New Town's force of mature streetwalkers while others sat waiting to retch in the New Town Jazz Cellars. Some slept on the steps of the hotel while friends and colleagues rested at the Police Station, Fire Station, the Rantings General Hospital, the Salvation Army Refuge and the New Town Dogs Home, while a wrestler was found asleep on top of the War Memorial.

Apart from the symphony of flushing toilets the New Town Hinchcliffe Hotel stood quiet and grey as matching daylight touched its top floors. On every room floor abandoned socks and shirts lay in a Customs Officer's delight. Doors open, lights left on, and the only sign of life: beards relentlessly growing on the pallid sleepers. The picture was repeated in every room.

Some of the famous, however, were not part of the carnival. They had gone to stay with friends. They were the Good Famous, who took nothing for nothing from no man unless he was an equal or better. Who were never seen to spit or heard belching. They were always clean and never blasphemed. Their brilliant sweaters were made for them by kind old ladies who also sent them cakes and photographs of their deceased husbands. The Good Famous had gone to bed early after nightcaps and a chat about old times. They lay breathing quietly by their wives in bedrooms as good as their own at home and would rise, fresh and lively, to enjoy a nourishing breakfast and then down to the golf club. It was good to have friends in The Rantings because all hotels these days were the same and one was hard put on waking and looking at the room to remember whether it was New York or Melbourne!

It was dawn, and in hotel and private home, in custody or out, the soldiers in the charity battle lay sleeping. On the battleground itself, with the ghostly tents and sponsors' banners flapping in their ears, the private security men smoked and checked this and tested that before returning to the fan heater in their hut. Some were out marching the course. There was always a loonie who liked to dig up a green before a big show, and they'd been warned about the Pringle family. No amount of warning was strong enough to prepare them for Adams's pig farm, of course, and day or night the stench was there like a beacon. The sky was growing lighter and there were scuds of dark cloud forming. The Barrier men were under strict instructions to ring Mr Jukes at any time if the weather looked to be turning nasty, but it was still a risky decision to make. Give it another half hour and if the sky grew dirtier they'd knock him up. The light went on in the Adams house and they marvelled that it didn't ignite the whole damn place. As the walkie-talkies crackled the day became bolder and it was clear that the cloud was definitely more dense and – hullo, here it comes!

'Barrier 2 to Barrier HQ. I'm over by the pig farm and it's started to rain. Over.'

'Barrier HQ. Thank you, Barrier 2. There's nothing here yet but the sky doesn't look promising. I'm contacting Mr Jukes. Over and out!'

Barrier 2 was drenched before he could replace the radio in his jacket, and hurried for the cover of Wayne's Wood. In the Barrier hut BHQ dialled Ralphie's number and waited.

'Hullo. Who the hell . . .'

'It's Barrier Security at the golf club, Mr Jukes.'

'Do you know what time it is, you silly bugger?'

'It's raining, Mr Jukes. Our lad out on the course reported rain a few minutes ago and it's tipping down all over now. Very heavy, and it looks like it's here to stay. Will you acknowledge that you have understood my message, please.'

Ralphie was sitting on the edge of his bed. 'Yes, I understand. What time is it?'

'0553 exactly. Jesus, did you hear that?' The line crackled and Ralphie winced. The lightning flickered and the low rumble of thunder bumped and bounded into the distance.

'Thanks. I'll be right over.' Ralphie cut off the conversation and dialled the Weather line. He never did understand Highs and Lows but the recorded announcement was encouragingly depressing. He replaced the phone and rubbed his hands. It was going to happen just the way he wanted it to. PLEASE let it piss down till at least the greens were flooded. Should he call Wing? Be nice to get him, especially if he was having an early heart-starter with the Hon. Philippa. No, not worth the bother. The old sod was coming to The Rantings later in the morning with old Kobiyashi on his first visit to Sheerpitts. It was time for a shave and a piece of toast and then across to the club.

He thought about an earlier call he had received from the hotel, which had shaken him a bit. At least three times as many as expected and the manager was billing him as Tournament Director, the little bastard! Pity it hadn't started raining yesterday before they set off. The manager had said they were like locusts. Good God, it hadn't been a mistake getting involved, had it? Steady, Ralphie, where's your bottle! At the end of the day the club would have to foot any bills and his rewards in commissions and backhanders would easily finance a fortnight on the Costa Mucho. What was he worrying about, it was raining! He went to the window. The rain thrashed against the glass and he could hardly see out. Its violence made him step back and he laughed as he turned towards the bathroom.

On the course, Barrier 4 was chasing a sponsor's banner and then gave up. The sodden cloth suddenly collapsed, waited for him and then, when he made a snatch at it, got up and ran away. He sighed and, shielding the radio with his shoulder, shouted into it:

'Barrier 4 to Barrier HQ. Another one's gone. The wind's getting up and it's just pulling them off the posts and blowing the buggers away. You're going to loose some marquees soon. I'm trying to save the banners but it's hopeless. Over.'

'Barrier HQ. You think you've got trouble, mate. The club's big hospitality tent has got about 5,000 gallons of water on its roof and it's going to split any moment. Try and save what you can, but if it gets worse you'd better come in. We haven't got a hovercraft. Barrier HQ out.'

The same message was sent to all eight of the private security experts attempting to fight wet canvas and they came in immediately. The rain was now falling horizontally and in Ralphie's car as he drove to the club the wipers simply altered the patterns on his windscreen. He was glad that it was so early and no traffic was about but he was still compelled to drive very slowly. The storm sounds had passed but the clouds continued to empty on to Sheerpitts and when Ralphie reached the club he felt, inspite of himself, a small pang of sympathy for those who had worked so hard on the tentage. The club's hospitality marquee, the biggest of all, was now crouching, giving birth to a ten-ton water baby. As he watched, the waters broke and he had to leap up the steps to avoid a tidal wave as it foamed past knocking over small inoffensive signs and tee boxes. It undermined the precisely defined setting of the grandstand scaffolding legs, and the structure swayed elegantly till it leant carefully against a tree and recomposed itself, groaning. He could see the security men running about doing nothing and the Dream Rantings housing estate came to mind. Oh my God, here he was praying for rain and his half-built homes for newly-weds were taking a hammering. He'd better ring Doreen later on, and find out how bad it was. The clubhouse doors were open and there were two security men sitting on members' chairs having a smoke. There was no point in bollocking them so he went past them with a brisk, 'Got nothing to do, then?'

At the New Town Hinchcliffe, the early calls were being ignored but loud thunder detonating overhead was having an effect on the near-dead and slowly they came face to face with their throbbing hangovers. The cisterns sang again and listlessly the day began to come alive. The pros and Celebrities sat on their beds staring dully at odd-shaped feet and wondering whether to shower before or after dressing. Every soul in the hotel said, 'Oh my God!' when they stood up and moved towards the bathroom. They said, 'Oh God!' standing over the pedestal and, 'AAAH!' when the cold water hit them. When it became warm, they stood as motionless as stick insects and let it run into gaping holes in their heads. They felt no better after a shower, and regardless of what kind of razor they used, all managed to sustain deep wounds. The women fared no better and rose after the men, looking even worse. None of them was playing and they would much rather have convalesced in their dishevelled beds, but they were given no peace. This was what they had come to Sheerpitts for, so let's get up to the club as we are honour-bound to do and give thanks that it's raining heavily.

To their mirrors the men said, 'There will be no golf today and we will be spared having to hack round with some self-important little fart intent on boring the maker's name off the ball before the 5th. Today is to be given over to recovery and then, after a couple of breaths of lunch, another precipitous leap into the ocean of alcohol. Our presence here has attracted the sponsorship and that's the whole point of charity. If we can have a bloody good time and make pots of dough for charity, where's the harm in keeping Scotland's only reason for existence on its feet. Come on, darling, aren't you ready yet? Bloody hell, you look awful! Get a bit of breakfast down you and you'll feel ten times worse. Come on, they'll all be down there . . .'

And they are. The staff, still shattered from the night before, are handing out wrong breakfasts and forgetting toast at every table. Every newspaper is open at the sports page, and when the toast and correct breakfast does arrive, it's a full Train Smash. Two eggs, sausage, bacon, mushrooms, black pudding, tomatoes, beans, hash browns and fried bread waiting for a thick application of ketchup. Tea and marmalade, more toast, swap a paper and then look at the watch. They say that Jukes chap is laying on transport and he's got cars leaving every fifteen minutes from the front. Just ask at Reception. I don't have to be on tee till elevenish so we're going to look around – what's this place called?

Ralphie had been talking to Sidlow for an hour and the Steward was nodding on auto. 'Don't open the bar till I tell you. Don't serve any meals till I tell you. Keep your eye on the policemen and if you see anyone, I don't care who it is, if you see anyone attempting to hit a golf ball in anger kill him instantly, do you understand? They went through town like a dose of salts last night and they've had a chance to recover, but keep them off the booze till I give you the word. Get Marilyn to serve tea and biscuits to everyone.

Where's Captain Hughton? Let me know when Sir Harold and the Shin Hai boss man turns up. Did you say the feller from the insurance company was here?' 'Yes, Mr Gerry Sansom.' 'Here's the first of them now.'

The first came in and shook hands warmly with everyone saying, 'What a shame about the weather, and after all the work you've put in, dear God I've got a throat like a Barcelona dustbin man's armpit. Any chance of a beverage, old chap? Ah, here's . . .'

Now they came in twos and threes and nines. Soon the clubhouse was full and there were still two hours before Sidlow was to serve lunch. The Brigadier shouted loudly, and for once all present agreed with him. What the hell was going on when the club was full of honoured guests and none of them was being insulted with a drink?

'Sidlow, get those damn towels off and do what you're paid for. Get the girl, for Gods' sake, we need something decent to look at in this bloody awful weather, and what are you having, old chap, that is, when the steward gets up off his fat arse! I must say that apart from the totally unnecessary and gratuitous violence you were very good in that ITV Police series, what was it called, and by jove we could do with you around here with that little sod Pringle . . . You weren't? You're a newsreader? Good Lord, thought that was a woman's job. Well, we all make mistakes. What's your handicap? Has anyone seen Ralphie? There he is! Ralphie, you've got to open the bar, old horse. Tell him, Hughton! Open the bar, Ralphie, or they'll tear the place to bits. They're much bigger than they look on telly!'

Now Ralphie speaks: 'For Christ's sake, Rhino, they'll drink us dry by one o'clock! We catered for 200-odd and there are thousands of the buggers. I didn't realize they were bringing their entire families and staff!'

'It gets worse, Ralphie! I hate to tell you but the punters are already making their way here from town. They came out of their little holes the moment the rain stopped. You must cancel officially and have the whole thing called off or we are in the mire up to our necks! Is that the sun coming out? Quickly, Ralphie, while they're still upright!'

'Ladies and gentlemen, I'm terribly sorry but . . . LADIES AND GENTLEMEN! Thank you. I'm afraid that the sun has arrived a little too late to save the day, so I'd like to thank you all for coming and there's transport provided for all those who wish to return to the hotel and make an early start home to beat the traffic, which I am told is building up horrendously. Ladies and gentlemen . . .'

'Give up, Ralphie, they are just not listening. No way is this lot going to shift. We'll have to dig out the PGA chap and get him to give it the chop. They might listen to him. Here's Sir Harold!'

'Harold, thank God you're here. Have you seen the tents?'

'Dear God, Ralphie, where is that idiot Dowty? One of his imbeciles . . . yes, Mr Kobiyashi, in there. Go in with him, Constable. That lunatic has just arrested Mr Kobiyashi!'

'Was that . . . ?'

'Yes, and the brainless moron who went in with him has just five minutes ago arrested him for indecent behaviour!'

'Calm down, Harold, and come into the office . . . Now, what happened?'

'I'll tell you what happened. You know the old man likes to stand naked in the driving rain to state his oneness with the game. That's all he was doing, and I couldn't very well stop him, could I? He is our bloody guest after all, and that cretin sprang up out of a bush and knocked him off! Ah, Mr Kobiyashi. This is the Tournament Director, Mr Kobiyashi. Mr Ralph Jukes. Pardon? Oh, I'm sure they'll find Mr Kinichiwa soon. Ralph, say "Hello."'

Blomberg's Progress

The final of the Vase Competition was a farce. It had to be with the pairing of Archie Gosling and Aaron Blomberg, for never in the history of the game did one player have such a tremendous advantage over his opponent. The plain and simple fact was that Gosling was the greatest golfer ever to have lived, and he was in thunderous practice form at the Beijing when Ah Wi Li, the small man serving him garupa fish in hot bean sauce, whispered that Mr Blomberg wished to play the Vase final early next morning, before the main tournament, to spare them both the horror and blistering embarrassment of performing in front of a gallery.

Wi Li would pick Archie up from whatever stupor he lay in and convey him to the course next morning. The reason for the small man's involvement in the scheme was that Blomberg was the only European who made less noise than a Cup Final crowd when eating at the Lotus Flower, and Ah was happy to help him on this occasion and pick up a free broad-checked bookie's suit for his trouble.

Early next morning, amidst the falling tents and driving rain, Archie stood on the 1st tee with the last remnants of bean sauce being washed out of his hair. He didn't notice the elements or the intoxicated duo who had joined Blomberg and himself in the semi-dark, and drove his ball to a spot 75 yards from the flag placed by Blomberg's brother Sol on the 1st green. After taking 19 strokes Aaron conceded and they moved onto the 2nd, slipping past the policemen watching the security men who were watching Isaac Blomberg whose job it was to deflect attention away from the flag planter. After the 6th Archie was beginning to sober up dangerously, and he unconsciously called on the instinct which even in his most confused state would lead him to the several whisky caches located near and about every hole. Aaron watched him lurch into the brook guarding Miss Woodley, after deliberately overhitting a superb second into the crescent of trees, and there grope anxiously for his lode. Moaning nervously he climbed out and went to the trees where the second deposit was concealed. Nothing was to be found in either!

By the 8th tee Gosling was paralytically sober, and walking miserably erect with a clear head and a nervous system functioning perfectly for the first time in decades. He felt the rain hitting him while dawn's light was pounding in through unusually wide-open eyes. He knew quite clearly that he was playing Blomberg and that he needed a drink. There were two other men staggering along with them and they looked like he wanted to be and couldn't. The blasted ball kept shooting off all over the place, and, by God! Blomberg had improved. He'd only taken 16 on the last to Archie's 20! At every hole the dimly remembered alcohol caches were rummaged for without success and he was reduced to casually observing that he had a thirst and did Jews carry a drink with them when they played?

Blomberg, who wasn't such a bad chap after all, said no but his hospitality tent, if it still stood, was liberally stocked and waiting for them on the 16th. From that moment Aaron began to play out of his skin. He was hitting the green under the dozen almost every hole, and Gosling's game had disintegrated to such a state that when his opponent slaughtered the 207-yard par-three 15th in a best-ever 12 strokes, Blomberg was 1 up with 3 to play! They had dropped their two shadows, who were sleeping by the Adams pig farm fence when they stood in the pelting rain on the Hell Hole tee, held up by the gusty wind on one side and the porcine effluvia on the other. For all the fat finalist noticed the stench, he could have been standing outside the main bottling stores for Chanel Number 5! He was on the brink of a legendary triumph to make up for Massada and all that had gone before or come after! The snide insults and hurtful slights, the sniggers at the bacon in his sausage rolls and the pigfat on the trolley axle.

Aaron's confidence was now majestic and Archie could only groan as his opponent's drive rolled on and on interminably until at last it stopped nearly 50 yards from the tee. Archie gritted his teeth, and thinking of the golden fluid waiting for him in the wrecked tent which he could see 212 yards away in the painfully bright light, he slashed viciously at the ball. Blomberg bit his lip in pity as the topped drive skittered away from the ugly scar and stopped within hailing distance. They fought their way through the weather to the green, Archie conceding hysterically as he ran to the tent. Aaron was 2 up with 2 to play. Inside Abraham Blomberg welcomed both players, inquired of their health and begged them to drink with him. His brother sank his fruit juice gratefully, but Gosling's fell from his shaking hand in a great orange fan. 'You prefer blackcurrant cordial?' Abraham asked, but he was talking to a broken man.

'Is there nothing else? A hip flask, a medical cabinet?'

'Iodine would kill you, Mr Gosling!' Aaron said and led him out. 'My honour, I think!' There was no need to play the last for after missing a half-inch putt on the 17th Archie sat down and began to cry as a helicopter flew over, the pilot shouting at them. Blomberg helped Archie to his feet and they walked back to the clubhouse where a large crowd was watching them and laughing soundlessly behind the windows.

'I just can't understand it,' said Archie. 'I'm sure there used to be whisky bottles all over the course. Didn't I use to hide them, Mr Blomberg?'

The victor could no longer see the man suffer. 'You should never trust workmen, my friend! That fellow who fell off the scaffolding when Mrs Gurning came? He fell on one of your collections! Every time they put up a tent they scoured the area. I would have brought a bottle but as you know we Blombergs do not drink!'

Aaron had wondered at first about the members' complaints concerning excessive conviviality amongst the scaffolders and their mates, but his sharp mind soon linked Gosling's buried treasure with the euphoria. A clandestine visit had confirmed his suspicions and offered him a perfectly legal way to win. 'Thank you, Mr Gosling, it was a joy to play against you . . .'

Aaron was talking to thin air as Archie raced ahead to get a drink. The Celebrities waved and joked at the sight but those members who witnessed the spectacle creased their brows in wonderment and concern, for nobody, however far back they thought, could remember Archie Gosling being able to stumble, never mind sprint like an Olympian! They watched him smash through the roadblock of policemen holding back the autograph seekers and plough to the bar sobbing, and turned to each other in horror. When their gaze returned to the window they could see Aaron Blomberg following at a measured pace, and when at last he passed before them on his way to the locker room he raised his rain-sodden panama at the very spot where they had laughed and hooted at him during the bizarre confrontation with Sam Cuddy.

'Er . . . hello. This is the Club Secretary. Rhino, find a blanket for Mr Kobiyashi! As for you, son, you're in big lumber! Don't you know who this gentleman is? It's only the boss-man of the company sponsoring most of today. Bloody hell, Marilyn, don't you ever knock? What? Oh for Gods' sake, alright, tell your Dad to open the bar! Nice girl, Mr Kobiyashi. Gents, if you'll excuse me for just a couple of phone calls . . . "Hello! Mr Dowty, please. It's very urgent. Ralphie Jukes at the golf . . . oh, he is. Thanks. Goodbye." He's on his way over, Harold. You'll be sorted out in no time. Mr K! I'll be with you in a sec. "Hello, I was given this number to ring at any time for Mr Gerry Sansom of SafeHaven . . . He's at Sheerpitts? That's fantastic! Ralphie Jukes. Yes, it's a terrible shame. Yes, we're all very upset. Yes. Thanks. Goodbye." Gerry's already here. He came over as soon as it became light! Good lad, he's the one who's going to save our dough. Well, fancy it raining like that, and then clearing up so quickly. Do you get anything like this in Japan, Mr Kobiyashi? Come in! Ken! Am I glad to see you! This is the Assistant Chief Constable, Mr Kobiyashi. Ken, Sir Harold wants a quiet . . .'

'Mr Dowty, I was bringing the senior management of Shin Hai Zips here this morning and en route the head of the company stopped to make his devotions . . .'

'Good morning, Sir. PC Finch, Sir, Sheerpitts Golf Club detail, Sir. He was bollock-naked, Sir . . .'

'Hop it, Sunshine, I'll speak to you later! I'm very sorry about this little misunderstanding, Mr Coffeehachi, and the officer will be dealt with. If in future you could worship indoors it might save us a great deal of trouble! I'm surprised at you, Sir Harold! Can I have a word outside with you, Mr Jukes? . . . Ralphie, old Hirohito in there is the least of my worries at the present. On the way here the station called to inform me that they had just received a call from the Charlie Twatface is Innocent nutcases alleging that they have placed a bomb on the course.'

'That's absolutely fan . . . I mean, SHIT! Ken, you'll have to clear the place! We can't have people's deaths on our consciences. Good God, it's only a charity!'

'It's a hoax, Ralphie! There's no bomb here. The only thing is, the bastards know that I can't take a chance and ignore the call.'

'That's right, Ken, clear the clubhouse immediately!'

'Now, now, Ralphie, it's not like you to panic, calm down! There's nothing in the building. My lads have been watching your security jokers all night, and believe me, the place is clean! The caller said that the bomb was on the course so all we have to do to stop this lot panicking is TELL 'EM NOTHING, and keep the course clear. I'm sending out a couple of my lads to bring that fourball in if they haven't finished already.'

'What fourball? There's nobody out there, Ken. There can't be!'

'My traffic helicopter was doing a bit of prowling early on and spotted them. Fat feller in a panama hat, and three others.'

'Blomberg! It was Blomberg! Oh no! Has anyone seen Archie Gosling? Rhino, look after things here while I . . .'

'What's up with Ralphie, Rhino?'

'He's carrying a lot of responsibility, Mr Dowty. Do you think our guest might like a cup of tea?'

'Brigadier, have you seen Archie? Colonel Beam, have you by any chance seen Blomberg with Archie in the club or outside? Murdo, have you seen Blomberg? Where? They weren't . . . Oh my God! Gerry! Where did you pop up from? Yes, what a disaster! I believe you've been here from the start. Thanks for being so punctilious, and I hope you'll push our claim through . . . Problems, old chap?'

'Ralphie, there's a fourball out there, and you know the stipulations of the policy!'

'Gerry, old lad, they're nothing to do with the Pro-Am! It's a private party. You know that mad bugger Blomberg? He's trying to finish the Vase competition . . .'

'It was a fourball, Mr Jukes! I recognized the big wrestler chap from ITV and the other one, I think, was that snooker player who always stays out at night, whatsisname?'

'Gerry, you're mistaken. I told everybody that it was off! That particular group was, I assure you, a private function and completely dissociated from . . .'

'That's what they all say when someone slips through the net and blows the Abandonment Policy, Mr Jukes. How do you think we in Insurance are going to earn our living if someone doesn't hear the recall gun? No, I shall make my report, and you will be hearing from head office within four days. Goodbye.'

'You bastard!' (Turns) 'You lot, did you hear that? That's how a Brother Mason treats you. Yes, you can turn your backs. You're all on the square, why didn't you give me a hand then? Get lost. Excuse me. Can I pass through? EXCUSE ME! Thank you. Jesus, Harold, we've lost the insurance cover! That sod Blomberg is out there with Archie Gosling – they must have picked up a couple of stop-outs to play with them – and Sansom is claiming that they've negated the policy!'

'I have always said, Ralph, that it's bad news letting them into a golf club, and I believe that you were instrumental in fixing Blomberg's membership here? Isn't there somewhere we can take Mr Kobiyashi? What about the Steward's flat? He needs a spot of peace and quiet and that crowd out there have turned the place into a bear garden! Get that young girl to look after him. Quickly, Ralphie, there's a lot at stake!'

As the day wore on the pace increased, but still the famous and the unknown shouted and slapped each other's shoulders and told each other what great chaps they were. Their wives became frivolous and whispered in complete strangers' ears. Couples disappeared, and when Tina Gurning walked in it was the only time on that memorable day when anything like silence was noticed. Ten Celebrities hunted her down and her instant success inspired Gerta Beam and Mrs Protheroe to walk through the crowded bar wantonly distributing cakes and tea.

Outside, the amorphous Rantonians, undeterred by intermittent squalls of rain, stood like a great defeated army gaping and gasping at the occasional glimpse of a notorious elbow at a window or the swift rush to a car for something. The police holding them back were in genial mood and the sounds from the clubhouse only served to show the watching punters how the great could enjoy themselves in such a grand manner.

Inside, Ralphie watched the frantic enjoyment with Hughton at his shoulder.

'What are you going to do about Blomberg?' asked the Secretary. 'He's cost the club a fortune.'

Ralphie shook his head wearily. 'I don't know. I just hope that he's so bucked to win, and we'll have to let the result stand, he'll be so happy that he might consider making some kind of donation. The bugger isn't short of a crust. Here! *They* aren't club members. How did they get in? Christ! That's Dolly Pringle, isn't it? That's all we need. Find Ken Dowty. He won't want telling twice.'

Hughton disappeared into the noise and Ralphie looked around. Terry Wogan was chatting pleasantly to Colonel Beam and Henry Cooper roared with laughter at something the Brigadier had suggested. Peter Alliss examined his feet while Murdo McNish was advocating Sandy Lyle's need to concentrate on a neat one-piece takeaway, make sure he got his weight onto his right side and then get through the ball. In his opinion he had come dangerously close to a reverse pivot with the weight remaining on the left foot and everything flying off to the right. He looked puzzled when Alliss mentioned the Dowager's Hump and excused himself. A happy clutch stood round Jimmy Tarbuck as the cheerful gap-toothed Liverpudlian regaled them with a fund of golfing gags and stories of his game with Bob Hope. Michael Caine had cried off at the last moment because of a film in Bali but Val Doonican stood, trapped by a ring of older lady members, smiling resolutely at the threat of more sweaters through the post. A man who could only be Ignacio de Leon was pinned to the wall near the glass doors by John Potts, the club's religious maniac, who was pointing out the sheer futility of the Pope's recent visit to Chile and the vile military dictatorship of the Junta.

Elsewhere, beleaguered by determined members, could be seen Bruce Forsyth, Frank Bruno, Sean Connery and Omar Sharif. They stood like infantry at Waterloo, attacked from all sides but kept upright by the animal press of their interrogators. Telly Savalas's glinting dome towered over Sidlow at the bar as he compared imperial measures to the miserly tots the Steward was dispensing. Everywhere that Ralphie's eyes rested was a face that came almost instantly to mind. Des O'Connor, Ronan Rafferty, Tony Jacklin, Sam Torrance, all trapped like butterflies in the public collection. The room and the doorways were absolutely packed and still more were coming in. Ralphie was sure that members of the public were somehow infiltrating and he nudged and butted his way through the bodies. Outside the weather was now that of high summer and the room temperature was becoming unpleasant. Pushing through the happy tangle he came face-to-face with Margaret Vyner-Kenty.

'I have just been talking to that man who was in the Bond films. He is disgusting and I have told him so. Women in those stupid, childish adventures are portrayed as nothing more than sex objects, and when I suggested that they should be given more thinking roles he said something about broccoli which appalled me. I think he should be asked to leave!'

Ralphie ignored her and allowed himself to be washed away to another raft where the Brigadier had moved on to the bulky figure of Ian Botham.

'Do you knock them all off? I used to be bit of a lad myself years ago. Ever holed in one? I've done it so often I've given up counting!'

Botham laughed and said, 'I believe so. They say you're the biggest cheat in the club, but this is such an awful bloody place I'd say they need bumptious old farts like you.'

'Exactly!' the Brigadier said raising his empty glass to the great all-rounder.

'Piss off and get your own,' the cricketer said without animosity and Patterson roared with laughter.

Ralphie gave up trying to get near the windows and bumped from one knot of drinkers to the next. On the Richter Scale the party could only be a whizz-banging success but he was worried about the approach of the Grand Dinner. The day was slipping by and it was only three hours before they were due to sit down for dinner. He turned as something hard and shiny caught the side of his head.

'We're giving up,' the police euphonium handler said disgustedly, 'the noise is too loud for us, Mr Jukes. I hope the Yanks have better luck. Colonel Ooks was looking for you. There he is over by the bar with Telly.'

He pointed ponderously with the massive horn and, taking advantage of the scattering bystanders, Ralphie made his way to the cluster round the bar.

'Oh Jesus, what a day!' he said to the Colonel.

'Hi, Ralphie. Telly, this is the guy I was telling you about. Hey, Ralphie, I'm sorry about my boys overflying just now. I'll kick ass for it because they were told to stay wide today. Shit, the moment they see a bit of sunshine you can't keep those mothers out of a F15.'

Ralphie nodded. He hated to tell the man that not one person in the clubhouse had been aware of the screaming noise blasting past mere feet above the roof.

'I was telling TS about Wayne. Isn't he something?'

Jukes smiled and tried to catch Sidlow's attention. Savalas came closer. 'You should watch this bum. His idea of a drink is not very generous. You could lose friends this way. That big guy who looks like a wrestler has just threatened to rip off his head!'

'I'll keep an eye on him,' Ralphie muttered. 'He's been trying that on for some time. Nice to meet you, Mr Savalas!'

'Likewise. Tough we couldn't get round today, Mr Jukes, but you got a good crowd of rubbernecks outside. You gonna make your dough?'

The Tournament Director affirmed with a head shake.

'That's what it's all about, cookie! Man, I am hungry. When do we eat, Mr Jukes?'

It was time for Ralphie to forget his drink and avoid further uncomfortable questions. 'I'm organizing that now, Mr Savalas, so if you'll allow me . . .' He waved apologetically and turned away.

'That's a helluva menu you got there, Ralphie,' he heard Colonel Ooks say. 'I can't wait to get to the trough with my friend here who is on a diet.'

'Like hell I am,' the bald one said and they turned back to the bar. Out of the crowd Nobosuke Kinichiwa loomed.

'Mr Jukes, have you heard about Mr Kobiyashi? He was arrested and beaten by one of your policemen!'

'Come and have a drink, Nobbie. I think you've got a slightly distorted report of the incident. Our policemen are wonderful.'

Kinichiwa came very close. 'No, Mr Jukes. I have spoken to Mr Kobiyashi and he says that the policeman touched him! Perhaps he did not know that no other person other than the bath attendants are allowed to touch our Chairman's person!'

Ralphie was getting tired of people asking him questions and piling their worries and problems on him when he was not in the best of spirits. 'Don't worry about it, Nobbie. It'll all get sorted out!'

But Kinichiwa was still worried. 'For our Chairman to lose face at a crucial time like this could be most humiliating, Mr Jukes.'

Ralphie drew a long breath and threw his cap into the sunset. 'Look, I'll tell you what, Nobosuke. Come and talk to a friend of mine. I'm sure he'll understand your concern and he'll probably have something to say that might be of interest. That's him over there. The little man. His name is Gerald Patterson. Go over and tell him who you are.'

Kinichiwa looked over to the Brigadier. 'Thank you, Mr Jukes. Let us hope that the unfortunate misunderstanding between our countries can be swiftly rectified.'

Ralphie closed his eyes and turned away as the Deputy Managing Director of Shin Hai Zips set out to meet the Brigadier. He melted into the crowd. Rhino appeared at his elbow.

'I found Dowty. He said eighteen of the Pringle family managed to get in with forged VIP tickets and he believes there may be more. He says we must check tonight's dinner invitations extra-carefully. That fellow Moxon from the brewery has just turned up with a load of extra wine. There's nothing left of the stuff we were going to drink tonight.'

Now at last Ralphie noticed that here and there small knots of drinkers were dissolving. Oh, thank God, perhaps they were going back to the hotel or to their friends' homes to change for dinner. As soon as most of them were clear he'd have a chance to see how bad the disaster was and spread his losses somehow. Yes, they definitely were making the noises that drinkers make when they are leaving their fellow topers to take a short nap, get changed and come back to square one to start drinking again. The density of the people in the room decreased and the drab masses outside moved forward through the genial police to offer scraps of paper for signature. Soon the room was empty enough to see Jack Burberry asleep on his private chair and Ralphie went over to look at him.

'Bloody 'ell, Jack. You've got it made. I work my balls off and you sit here snoozing through hell and high water. Perhaps I've got it all wrong.'

The last of the Celebrities left and Ralphie surveyed the débris. The carpets was thickly worked with a mix of crushed biscuit, canapés and spilled everything. No table or flat surface did not bristle with glasses and the ashtrays had peaks of cigar stubs and crisp bags. Sidlow was opening the windows and every time he touched a solid object he groaned loudly. He saw Ralphie and came over holding his wrist out for show.

'Did you see what that bastard did to me? Tell him, Renée!'

Renée appeared by his side holding a dozen dirty glasses. 'That wrestler from television. He said Arthur was giving him short measure and gave him an Irish Whip or something. He's broken his wrist. You've got to do something, Mr Jukes . . . and the looks he was giving our Marilyn!'

'For Christ's sake, Arthur, you should have more sense than to serve them short. People are worse with free drink than they are with the stuff they pay for. Go and see McNish. Tell him I'd be obliged if he'd fix you up.'

Sidlow was happy to carry on complaining but Hughton was nearby and

intervened. 'McNish is outside attending to Mr Kinichiwa,' he said. 'By the main door. Come on, Sidlow, there's a lot to be done before tonight's big dinner.' The Sidlows left grumbling and Renée deposited the glasses angrily on the bar en route.

Returning to Ralphie's side the Secretary reported, 'Kinichiwa seems to have lost several teeth, Ralphie. The Japs aren't having a very good day, are they?'

'Bugger 'em. The money's in the bank. What happened to Nobbie? Not the Brigadier?'

Hughton nodded happily. 'Chinned him. Went out like a light. McNish is suggesting he takes a few days off at that private clinic he runs.'

The Tournament Director spread his hands. 'Just look at this lot. We've got to get everything ready for tonight. Has Ernie Dagwood showed up yet?'

Hughton gestured towards the kitchen. 'That's what really upset Renée Sidlow. He came in and just took over the place, which pissed her off more than a little.' He followed Ralphie through the wreckage to where the master caterer was assembling the final event of the Sheerpitts day.

Ernie Dagwood was approaching hysteria. 'What are the police talking about, the tents have blown down! I shall need a large marquee to finalize my preparations. Naturally in outside catering we are trained to expect anything, and last night's storm was nothing, but I *must* have somewhere to instruct my staff. This is impossible, Mr Jukes. You promised me . . .'

'I can't control the bloody weather, Ernie! You'll just have to do the best you can. Good God, that lot are so pissed you could give them fish and chips and they wouldn't know it.'

Dagwood's eyes narrowed and he became menacingly calm. 'That is not the point. I am an artist and food is my craft. You must give me space and I will provide a dinner *indimenticabile!*'

Hughton intervened. 'Mr Dagwood, we are somewhat limited for space at the moment. There are no tents and the best we can offer is the television lounge cum committee room which adjoins the dining room. Why don't we go and give it a once-over. In the Navy we always had to make bricks out of straw. This way, Mr Dagwood.'

Unbalanced by Hughton's reason the three made their way to the lounge and checked spaces and distances and all the other secrets necessary for a king of the kitchen to launch a superb meal from an emergency pad. They looked at spaces to stack plates and cutlery, for secure moorings for great tanks of soup, and for a shamefaced spot to hold Moxon's disgusting replacement wine. They watched Dagwood and could tell that, like any good cook, he was enjoying their attention and his own agony. At last he took out his handkerchief and said, 'It can be done, but only Dagwood could do it! Now leave me for I must think and re-think. Go!'

They went.

As Dagwood stood hand on hip at the golf club, the New Town Hinchcliffe was silent for the second time under Celebrity occupation. Each room held partially clothed sleeping figures stealthily preparing for the next stage of the Pro-Am weekend. The same was true of those who lodged with their friends, for the Good and Bad Famous all agreed on one thing, and that was that the dinner which capped every charity weekend was the highspot of the affair and they all should be there. They would awake as one and mysteriously assemble in dinner suit and cocktail dress waiting to be picked up, and brought home much later in shop-soiled condition. While Dagwood and his minions scurried through the clubhouse with collapsible tables and mountains of snowy linen, the sleepers' recovery period peaked and they began to stir. Soon they were repeating the morning's actions only with less stiffness and a definite aim in mind. She helped him with his cufflinks and he roughly zipped up the back of her dress. He stood by the window impatiently watching the mundane that passed for normal in The Rantings while she searched for the perfume and earrings. Just before they reached the brink of a row, she stood, smoothed down her dress and asked, 'How do I look?' 'You look great. Come on, for God's sake! Let's have one before we go.' And Hinchcliffe's Hideaway would be as full as the night before but not as noisy.

Then the cars pulled up and they surged eagerly out past the same stupefied Rantonians who had stared at them from every possible vantage point since their arrival. The cars plied smoothly forth and back with each driver asking for an autograph for his family. At the clubhouse, although they entered the same building by the same doors as they had in the morning, and were greeted by the same people, the dinner suits lent a different aspect to the manoeuvre and there was hushed solemnity brought on by tight collars and corsets as the men congealed at the bar and the ladies sat fiddling with their small evening bags. Dagwood's chefs, seen scuttling in the distance, brought with them the billowing odours of the seafood and overpowering sauces, and all set themselves on the starting blocks waiting only for Mr Kobiyashi, Sir Harold Wing, and the Lord and Lady Mayor. There was a drop in the hum of gossip and all eyes turned to the door where Jack Burberry, Ralphie, Margaret Vyner-Kenty and Len Gurning fluttered in a selfconscious cloud around the VIPs creeping into the room.

The Mayor, Raymond Bunn, and his wife Emily came in first, followed by Mr Kobiyashi and his minute spouse whom he did not introduce. She wore a traditional kimono and, standing by Emily in her flowered print, looked like an Elastoplast next to a badly bandaged wound. They made their way to the bar and stared dully while Sir Harold charmed everyone with stories that nobody but he understood. Looking deep into his first drink of the day (for safety), Ralphie was sunk in matters of profit and loss, mainly loss, when Wing nudged him to draw his attention to Ernie Dagwood who was signalling that all was ready.

'Well,' Ralphie said brightly, 'I'm glad that Mr Kinichiwa is feeling better after his fall. I do believe that is Mr Dagwood waiting to announce dinner!'

He nodded and Dagwood said, in a toastmaster's voice, 'Mesdames, messieurs, s'il vous plaît!' and dramatically indicated that the room, which they could see was full of chairs and had many tables laden with cutlery and porcelain, was indeed where they could expect to eat.

Ralphie grabbed the Mayor's thick arm. 'We go last, Ray. They clap us in!'

'That feller's on TV, Emily. He does that quiz game! Bloody waste of time!'

The handbags were gathered and ladies took gentlemen's arms and made for the dining room door where they gathered in a confused mob by the badly located seating plan. The strangulation dissembled after a few minutes and Ralphie matched the Mayor up with Mrs Kobiyashi, Emily Bunn with Mr K and Margaret Vyner-Kenty with Sir Harold. He brought up the rear with Len Gurning, who still smelled of wet sacks after a leaky night in the greenkeeper's hut. They entered to a dirge of clapping and peered for some time at the place names before Raymond Bunn sat in Ralphie's place and the Tournament Director was left without a seat. There were no further places on the top table and Jukes was looking round for Dagwood when Terry Wogan tugged his sleeve and said, 'I don't want to cause any trouble, Ralphie, but there's no place for a poor Irish lad and his little lady! We'll sit on the floor if you can find us a knife and fork!'

Ralphie could see a queue of familiar faces from all walks of entertainment and sport waiting behind the kindly Irishman, and his heart crumbled. To some of those without a place to rest this had happened before and they accepted it with Wogan's soft understanding, but others were not blessed with such humlity. 'I like to eat sitting down,' said Ignacio de Leon in perfect English. 'I want a seat or I must leave and catch a train which has seats for people like me!'

Dagwood appeared in a distressed condition. 'Mr Jukes, there are exactly 244 places set, as you ordered. If you would like to count . . .'

'Get some more seats,' Ralphie hissed. 'We'll just have to budge up and make more room at each table. We've got extra guests in, so find some chairs. I'll square you later, Ernie!'

He pushed the caterer away and raised his arms. 'I'm sorry about this, ladies and gentlemen, but there's been some kind of mix-up with the seating. We're laying some extra places so if you'd be patient for a little while longer . . .'

In the kitchen the *Tomates Farcies* began to merge with their neighbouring *Crevettes* while the *Consommé en Gelée* was now able to support a serving spoon quite comfortably. A procession of waiters and kitchen staff carried chairs pillaged from every part of the clubhouse into the dining room, all the time casting worried glances at the temporary kitchen relay station. The addition of 38 extra seats compelled the diners to a more intimate relationship with fellow gourmets than they would have wished, and when Ernie signalled briskly for the first course and its accompanying wine to be served, the difficulties soon became apparent.

Sean Connery's table solved theirs by alternately moving like two boat race teams, forward and back. Other tables followed, but what began with high jocularity ended in riotous spillage. Mr Kobiyashi and his tiny wife regarded the process with curiosity and tried to emulate Table 6 out of good manners and courtesy but found it too difficult without chopsticks and went back to staring helplessly at the sea urchins which Ralphie had ordered specially for them. Sir Harold was still smiling at Ralphie, but both men were thinking, 'Who the hell are these extra people? How can there be so many unexpected guests?' And while the MP was still genuinely puzzled a terrible truth was picking its way through Ralphie's ragged confidence.

'Christ, it can't be the bloody Pringles!' he said out loud. He stood up just as the waitress serving the Assistant Chief Constable screamed, 'Charlie is as Innocent as this *Gougère au Poulet* was when it was shot!' and tipped the lot over Dowty's head. Nyrene Pringle then removed her apron and black dress to reveal a generous figure covered only by a suspender belt and black stockings. She leapt over the table onto Dowty's lap in time for her brother to remove a camera from under his blonde wig and take a series of incriminating shots. Many thought that the episode was part of a surprise cabaret and Telly Savalas offered his head for the *Thon à la Provençale*, but others leapt to their feet aghast.

'I find this sort of thing disgusting!' yelled Jimmy Tarbuck, 'I came here to play golf not take part in blood sports!' and looking round for support found it coming only from Margaret Vyner-Kenty to whom he had taken a blistering dislike at first sight. He hurled his bread roll at her and ducked hurriedly as she reciprocated with a fishknife.

'You bitch!' Dowty shouted at Nyrene Pringle and tipped his cargo onto the floor where she lay rubbing her elbow and crying. 'I'll lock up every bloody one of your useless family!' He sprang to his feet. 'Right! Everyone stay in your seats while I get my lads to nail this crowd of loonies. Don't anyone move!'

Val Doonican, normally the mildest of men, rose to his feet amongst the bewildered guests and bogus waiters. He smiled, and speaking in the soft brogue of his native land said, 'Don't tell us what to do, feller. We're guests here and that looked like a pure accident to me.'

Several of the guests mischievously encouraged his natural good nature, infuriating the police beyond tolerance. 'Right, you're under arrest for obstructing a police officer!' shouted Dowty. He moved towards the gentle Celt who held his hands out in front of him in a saintly martyred gesture, but Dowty was heading for the door and the nearest police officer's radio. Then Doonican, trying to undo any harm he may unwittingly have caused, accidentally poked his finger in Gerald Patterson's eye. The Brigadier picked up his chair and in attempting to floor the singer caught Ignacio de

Leon on the back of the knee. The fiery Latin sprang to his feet, forgetting
that on sitting down at table he had discovered that his fly was undone;
while zipping it up he had caught the edge of the tablecloth between the
runners of the zip. Any normal zip would have released the tablecloth under
such urgent pressure, but this was a Shin Hai zip and took the tablecloth
with it. When de Leon finally collapsed under the strain, the table, its
contents and Tony Jacklin came down on top of him. The Brigadier,
thinking he was being attacked in the rear, swung his chair in a wide arc and
was delighted to catch the Lady Captain as she tried to throttle Des
O'Connor who had simply asked her what was going on. Gerta Beam looked
at her husband, who was watching the brawling with acid distaste, and
carefully poured a glass of iced water over his rounded skull. In the middle of
the floor Ernie Dagwood stood paralyzed with horror as his master meal
turned into a custard-pie fight.

Amongst the guests, feelings were mixed for while the showbiz stars rose
to such an occasion and saw everything as a story to be filed away and told
another time, the sports stars played safe fearing permanent injury, and
when they fell or were pushed to the ground feigned death. Ralphie shrieked
at the top of his voice but not a soul heard him except the grinning Hughton
who gave a jolly thumbs-up before going down under Nicholas Parsons, a
surprise last-minute Celebrity. The Tournament Director only stopped
screaming when Dowty returned with The Rantings Special Snatch Squad
and pointed him out as the first target. He did not see Mr Kobiyashi drop the
first three officers who attempted to escort him to safety, or Mrs Kobiyashi
repeat the exercise with her escorts. He also missed Archie Gosling who,
incoherently drunk, walked through the struggling mass untouched and out
onto the patio where he fell over the wall and went to sleep.

Sir Harold got out as he always did and nobody really tried to stop Frank
Bruno or Sean Connery. Everyone had a go at Des O'Connor, and the police
left the Brigadier and Margaret Vyner-Kenty to fight for some time before
they moved in. Each person, when taken into custody or escorted to friends'
homes or the New Town Hinchcliffe, was asked if they would like to make
a statement. Some did and others declined. When faced by the desk sergeant
at New Town Police Station later that night, Brigadier Gerald Patterson
stood to attention and said without any sign of remorse:

'Brush your teeth with Snelgrove
Clean your feet with Snelgrove
Wash your bum with Snelgrove every day
Snelgrove helps you work, dance,
                  sing,
                  cough,
                  whistle,
                  fart and play.'

THE AFTERMATH

'Aft-errr the ball was o-verrr . . .'

A lot of people in The Rantings said that Sheerpitts Golf Club would never be the same after the Pro-Am, but it was. Some of the participants in the fiasco changed, but people always do change and most of them don't need a fiasco to initiate the process. The club today is identical to the Sheerpitts of yesterday. The Irishman still delivers potatoes and they are eaten by new faces, but while some features are different the jobs and attitudes which cause them to smile or frown are the same.

Nobody from the New Town comes near the place. Dear Old Jack Burberry died sitting in his favourite chair at the club, and sat there for all of Bank Holiday Monday and a little of the Tuesday before the new steward noticed. Sidlow would have spotted Jack's demise much faster because he was a very sharp man. He was so sharp that he ended up in the same cell as 'Charlie is Innocent' Pringle. You'd have thought that having his wrist broken at the Pro-Am would have taught him a lesson but it didn't, and along with George Moxon he tried to do a fiddle over the big Wake for Dear Old Jack.

If anything, Ken Dowty is even more paranoid now that he has resigned his membership but he still visits Sheerpitts regularly, though rarely on his own. Mostly he arrives in the company of twenty other officers who are teetotallers and keen observers of the laws that govern the sale of liquor, gaming, suspicious substances and living off immoral earnings. Arthur Ransome Sidlow and George Moxon both went down when the brewery became suspicious about the amounts of alcohol being consumed, and a chance remark by a member concerning the extortionate size of the club's bill from the Rantings Water Board. Renée Sidlow is now the manager's wife at the Rest and Be Buggered which, although packed as ever with monumentally dull bookbinders and teachers, now has a *frisson* of sexuality in the air when Renée sometimes goes OTT on a Saturday night.

Captain Rhino Hughton remains Club Secretary. The barking laugh and tremendous delight at the discomfort of others still keep him out of the Masonic Order, and now he is the only surviving member of the Old Guard. The Brigadier damaged his head when venting his fury on Nobosuke Kinichiwa and became ill, calling out constantly for his dog. He died three months after the Pro-Am and left a note bequeathing part of his anatomy to Sheerpitts Golf Club. Not being in the spare-parts business, the General Purposes Committee accepted the bequest reluctantly but out of relief at getting rid of its original owner. When Gerald's artificial leg arrived in a

glass case there was great consternation that the dwarf had deceived them for so long, and one night it was buried near the plaque on the green covering Bagyard-Dawes's dead monopeds.

Greenkeeper Moorcock disappeared during the storm and was never seen again. Len Gurning, who was sleeping under his sacks during the height of the tempest, thinks that he was awakened during the frenzy by Moorcock bending over him and saying that he was going outside and that he might be gone for some time. Tina Gurning was reputed to have met her match in the fury of the storm with Wayne Summers, and her husband Len now spends two nights per week at home, though when there he sleeps under sacks in his greenhouse.

Wayne and Marilyn had talks during the Pro-Am with an Independent Film Producer who pointed out their path to fame and fortune if they would consider appearing in some Adult films he had in mind for the Middle East market. They were both deeply offended and gave it a try. Marilyn can have anything she wants from Tyre to Rabat, and a special golf course is being laid out for her partner in the Djebel Amour.

The Lady Captain renounced her membership when the Wimmins Ranting Golf Club opened its doors a year after the Shin Hai affair. There she was utterly dominated by wimmin twenty times tougher than herself, and many were the times she longed for a chance to heap abuse upon disgusting pigs like Archie Gosling. He drinks on, and plays blinding golf in all weathers if sustained by the amber fluid, and is completely forgiven for the Blomberg aberration. Norman Cooper was persuaded not to retire and he still complains, drinks, overcharges and leans heavily on the new assistant professional, a spotty youth who sadly cannot maintain the standards set by Wayne Summers. Mrs Protheroe and the female spectrum often yarn about what happened between the gilded youth and everyone but themselves, and there is a wistfulness in their eyes when they enlighten new lady members on what would happen if they went down to the woods today.

Everyone was furious with Aaron Blomberg when his name went up on the Honours' Board, but he was just glad to see it up there, and there is a strong chance that Abraham and Sol Blomberg may be allowed in as Artisans next year if Aaron's new club blazer scheme is passed by the Committee.

When the smoke of the Grand Dinner uproar cleared and the figures were all totted up, there was enough to clear the club's expenses and re-stock the bar. Ralphie, however, received a hammering from the members of Sheerpitts and was forced to resign. He was crushed . . . for twenty minutes, and then he jumped into the Jag and over a cup of coffee with Colonel Ooks diverted seven tons of prohibited Hair Gel to Teheran in return for three magnificent rugs to enrich the Blomberg home. Ralphie pops across to the Costa Bandito now and then to spend warm nights with Nyrene Pringle who impressed him greatly when she posed as a waitress at the Grand Dinner. Charlie will be out soon. The campaign for his release petered out when Dowty left the club, but if anyone could find the camera which took the pictures of Nyrene, semi-naked on the policeman's lap, and which was lost in the mêlée . . .

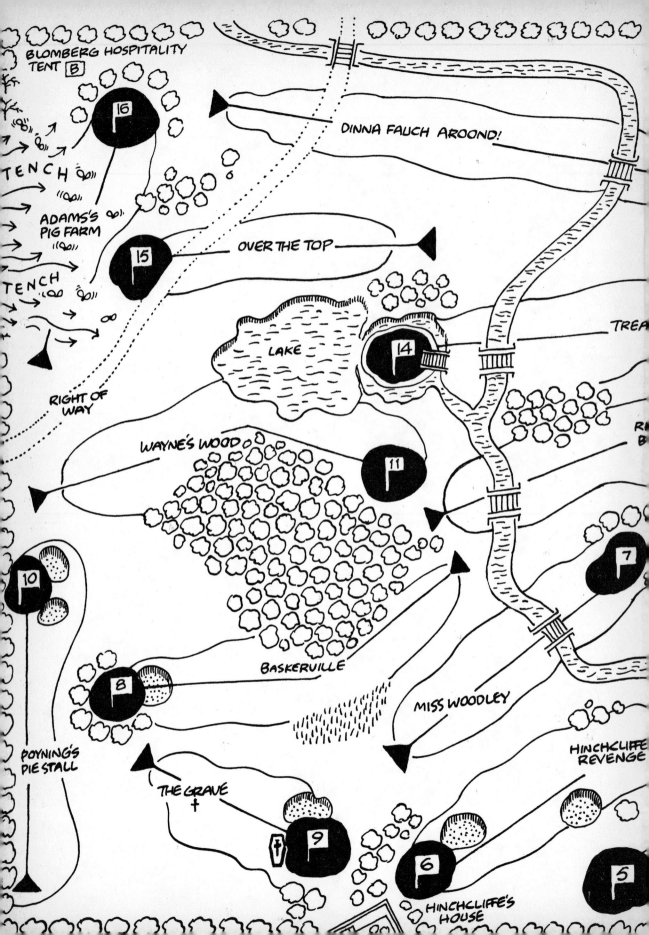

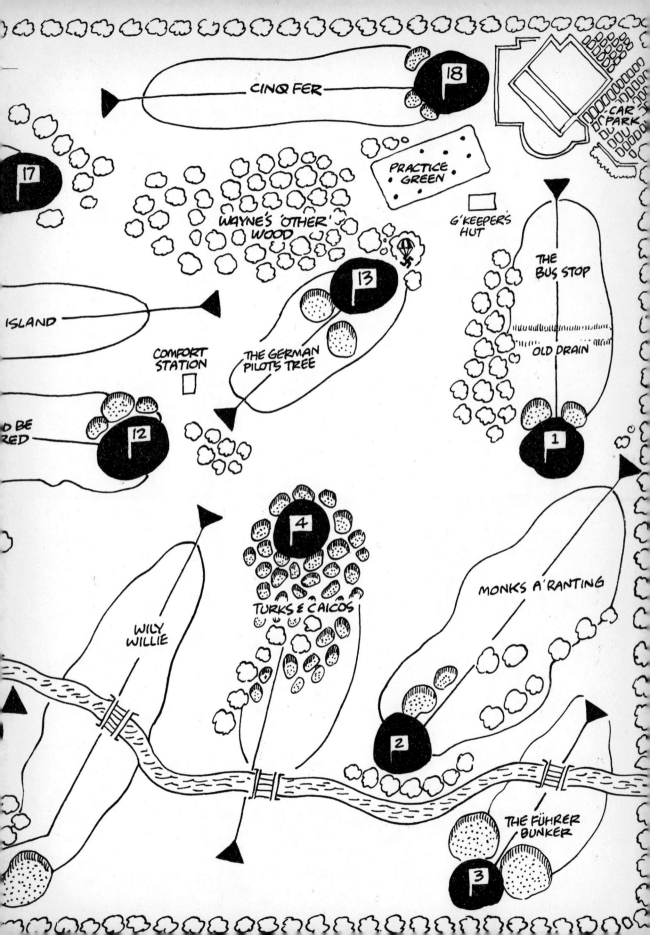